HOUGHTON MIFFLIN
HISTORY-SOCIAL SCIENCE
★ NEIGHBORHOODS ★

California
Home Connection Guide

An exciting year is ahead of you. You'll learn
about people and places, in the past and today.

Welcome!

to History-Social Science

Dear Student and Family,

What were families like in the past? How does a grape become a raisin? Who was Sitting Bull? For some answers, you could write a whole book!

This year you will learn so much. You'll read about brave actions, tough decisions, and great ideas, past and present. You'll read maps and stories, and biographies.

What do these tell you about people long ago and today? Let's find out together.

You, your teacher, and your textbook, along with exciting activities you can do with your classmates and your family—all will bring you learning success.

CALIFORNIA

Learning at Home . . .

How can family members make a difference?

1   **Get to know the content standards for Grade 2.** History-Social Science standards include history, geography, economics, good citizenship, and current events. The standards are learning goals. They will help you learn skills and understand what is important to remember.

2   **Read, observe, explore!** Be involved. Your family can use the Home Activities Checklist shown here. There are many ways to support learning at home all year.

Home Activities Checklist

☑ Read together and talk about text that informs, such as newspapers, biographies, and nonfiction.

☑ Use the library and talk to the librarian about topics of interest.

☑ Share positive stories about your family's history—people, places, events—through description or actual materials.

☑ Look for opportunities daily to talk about geography. Use local maps together. Use maps to locate places where you and other family members have lived.

☑ Easy economics! What is needed and what does it cost? Economics is all around you.

☑ Go over school work and support school projects and activities.

California Content Standards

Students differentiate between things that happened long ago and things that happened yesterday.

1. Trace the history of a family through the use of primary and secondary sources, including artifacts, photographs, interviews, and documents.

2. Compare and contrast their daily lives with those of their parents, grandparents, and/or guardians.

3. Place important events in their lives in the order in which they occurred (e.g., on a time line or storyboard).

2.2 Students demonstrate map skills by describing the absolute and relative locations of people, places, and environments.

1. Locate on a simple letter-number grid system the specific locations and geographic features in their neighborhood or community (e.g., map of the classroom, the school).

2. Label from memory a simple map of the North American continent, including the countries, oceans, Great Lakes, major rivers, and mountain ranges. Identify the essential map elements: title, legend, directional indicator, scale, and date.

3. Locate on a map where their ancestors live(d), telling when the family moved to the local community and how and why they made the trip.

4. Compare and contrast basic land use in urban, suburban, and rural environments in California.

2.3 Students explain governmental institutions and practices in the United States and other countries.

1. Explain how the United States and other countries make laws, carry out laws, determine whether laws have been violated, and punish wrongdoers.

2. Describe the ways in which groups and nations interact with one another to try to resolve problems in such areas as trade, cultural contacts, treaties, diplomacy, and military force.

2.4 Students understand basic economic concepts and their individual roles in the economy and demonstrate basic economic reasoning skills.

1. Describe food production and consumption long ago and today, including the roles of farmers, processors, distributors, weather, and land and water resources.

2. Understand the role and interdependence of buyers (consumers) and sellers (producers) of goods and services.

3. Understand how limits on resources affect production and consumption (what to produce and what to consume).

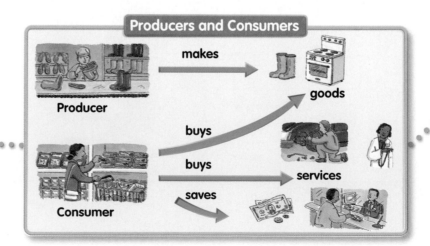

2.5 Students understand the importance of individual action and character and explain how heroes from long ago and the recent past have made a difference in others' lives (e.g., from biographies of Abraham Lincoln, Louis Pasteur, Sitting Bull, George Washington Carver, Marie Curie, Albert Einstein, Golda Meir, Jackie Robinson, Sally Ride).

Abraham Lincoln

George Washington

Historical and Social Sciences Analysis Skills

Chronological and Spatial Thinking

1. Students place key events and people of the historical era they are studying in a chronological sequence and within a spatial context; they interpret time lines.

2. Students correcly apply terms related to time, including *past, present, future, decade, century,* and *generation.*

3. Students explain how the present is connected to the past, identifying both similarities and differences between the two, and how some things change over time and some things stay the same.

4. Students use map and globe skills to determine the absolute locations of places and interpret information available through a map's or globe's legend, scale, and symbolic representations.

5. Students judge the significance of the relative location of a place (e.g., proximity to a harbor, or trade routes) and analyze how relative advantages or disadvantages can change over time.

Research, Evidence, and Point of View

1. Students differentiate between primary and secondary sources.

2. Students pose relevant questions about events they encounter in historical documents, eyewitness accounts, oral histories, letters, diaries, artifacts, photographs, maps, artworks, and architecture.

3. Students distinguish fact from fiction by comparing documentary sources on historical figures and events with fictionalized characters and events.

Historical Interpretation

1. Students summarize the key events of the era they are studying and explain the historical context of those events.

2. Students identify the human and physical characteristics of the places they are studying and explain how those features form the unique character of those places.

3. Students identify and interpret the multiple causes and effects of historical events.

4. Students conduct cost-benefit analyses of historical and current events.

HOUGHTON MIFFLIN
HISTORY-SOCIAL SCIENCE

★ NEIGHBORHOODS ★

Visit **Education Place**®
www.eduplace.com/kids

CALIFORNIA

★ AUTHORS ★

Senior Author
Dr. Herman J. Viola
Curator Emeritus
Smithsonian Institution

Dr. Cheryl Jennings
Project Director
Florida Institute of
   Education
University of North Florida

Dr. Sarah Witham
Bednarz
Associate Professor,
   Geography
Texas A&M University

Dr. Mark C. Schug
Professor and Director
Center for Economic
   Education
University of Wisconsin,
   Milwaukee

Dr. Carlos E. Cortés
Professor Emeritus, History
University of California,
   Riverside

Dr. Charles S. White
Associate Professor,
School of Education
Boston University

Consulting Authors
Dr. Dolores Beltran
Assistant Professor
Curriculum Instruction
California State University, Los Angeles
(Support for English Language Learners)

Dr. MaryEllen Vogt
Co-Director
California State University Center for
the Advancement of Reading
(Reading in the Content Area)

HOUGHTON MIFFLIN
HISTORY-SOCIAL SCIENCE

★ NEIGHBORHOODS ★

HOUGHTON MIFFLIN   BOSTON

CALIFORNIA

Consultants

Philip J. Deloria
Associate Professor
Department of History
and Program in
American Studies
University of Michigan

Lucien Ellington
UC Professor of Education
and Asia Program
Co-Director
University of Tennessee,
Chattanooga

Thelma Wills Foote
Associate Professor
University of California,
Irvine

Stephen J. Fugita
Distinguished Professor
Psychology and Ethnic
Studies
Santa Clara University

Charles C. Haynes
Senior Scholar
First Amendment Center

Ted Hemmingway
Professor of History
The Florida Agricultural &
Mechanical University

Douglas Monroy
Professor of History
The Colorado College

Lynette K. Oshima
Assistant Professor
Department of Language,
Literacy and Sociocultural
Studies and Social Studies
Program Coordinator
University of New Mexico

Jeffrey Strickland
Assistant Professor, History
University of Texas Pan
American

Clifford E. Trafzer
Professor of History and
American Indian Studies
University of California,
Riverside

Teacher Reviewers

The publisher expresses gratitude to these and the many other California educators who participated in the development of this program.

Patrick Butler
Terrace View Elementary
Grand Terrace, CA

Becki Dios
Toro Park Elementary
Salinas, CA

Charmian Francis
Maie Ellis Elementary
Fallbrook, CA

Melanie Gates
John Burroughs Elementary
Long Beach, CA

Jo Ann Gillespie
Argonaut Elementary
Saratoga, CA

Conchita Lizardi
Antelope Meadows
Elementary
Antelope, CA

Shari Megaw
Central Elementary
Ontario, CA

Tammy Morici
Piñon Hills Elementary
Piñon Hills, CA

Kristen Werk
Parkside Elementary
Pittsburg, CA

Diana Williams
Callison Elementary
Vacaville, CA

History-Social Science Content Standards for California Public Schools reproduced by permission,
California Department of Education, CDE Press, 1430 N Street, Suite 3207, Sacramento, CA 95814.

Printed in the U.S.A.
ISBN: 978-0-618-42381-1
ISBN: 0-618-42381-8

56789-VH-13 12 11 10 09 08 07

Contents

Introduction

▷ **About Your Textbook** 14

▷ **Reading History-Social Science** 18

▷ **History-Social Science: Why It Matters** 20

Bringing the world to your classroom!

UNIT 1   People and Places   22

Vocabulary Preview
Reading Strategies: Summarize, Predict/Infer 24

Lesson 1 | Core   **All Kinds of Groups** 26
Extend   Literature — **"Recess Rules"** 30

   Map and Globe Skill Review Maps, Globes, Symbols,
Directions 32

Lesson 2 | Core   **Living Together** 36
Extend   Biography — Maggie Cervantes 40

   Map and Globe Skill Use a Grid 42

Lesson 3 | Core   **Cities and Suburbs** 44
Extend   History — A City Grows Taller 48

   Graph and Chart Skill Read a Calendar 50

Lesson 4 | Core   **Rural Communities** 52
Extend   Economics — Markets 56

Unit 1 Review   **Current Events Project** 58

UNIT 2 Places Near and Far

62

Vocabulary Preview
Reading Strategies: Question, Monitor/Clarify 64

Lesson 1
Core — **Your Address** 66
Extend — Biography — Sally Ride 70

Map and Globe Skill Parts of a Globe 72

Lesson 2
Core — **Land and Water** 74
Extend — Literature — The Great Smokies 80

Map and Globe Skill Use Intermediate Directions . . . 82

Lesson 3
Core — **Weather and Climate** 84
Extend — Readers' Theater — Big Storm Coming 88

Lesson 4
Core — **Regions** 92
Extend — Geography — Languages of Switzerland 96

Reading/Thinking Skill Identify Main Idea and Details . . 98

Lesson 5
Core — **Resources** 100
Extend — Literature — "Maple Talk" 106

Unit 2 Review Current Events Project 108

UNIT 3 Ways of Living

Vocabulary Preview
Reading Strategies: Summarize, Predict/Infer 114

Lesson 1 | Core | **Families from Many Places** 116
| Extend | **Primary Source** — Immigrants at Ellis Island . 122

Graph and Chart Skill Read a Timeline 124

Lesson 2 | Core | **Sharing Cultures** 126
| Extend | **Citizenship** — Yo-Yo Ma 132

Study Skill Conduct an Interview 134

Lesson 3 | Core | **America's Symbols** 136
| Extend | **Literature** — "The Star-Spangled Banner" . . . 142

Lesson 4 | Core | **We Celebrate Holidays** 144
| Extend | **Biography** — Cesar Chavez 148

Citizenship Skill Make a Decision 150

Unit 3 Review Current Events Project 152

UNIT 4 | People at Work

Vocabulary Preview
Reading Strategies: Question, Summarize 158

Lesson 1 | Core   **Needs, Wants, and Choices** 160
| Extend   **Literature** — The Milkmaid 162

     Reading/Thinking Skill Compare Fact and Fiction . . . 164

Lesson 2 | Core   **Work** 166
| Extend   **History** — First Farmers 170

Lesson 3 | Core   **Goods and Services** 172
| Extend   **Biography** — Scientists Serving Others 174

     Graph and Chart Skill Read a Bar Graph 178

Lesson 4 | Core   **People Save Money** 180
| Extend   **Economics** — Spend Your Dollar 184

     Study Skill Use Reference Books 186

Lesson 5 | Core   **From Field to Market** 188
| Extend   **History** — Keeping Food Cold 194

Lesson 6 | Core   **People and Nations Trade** 196
| Extend   **Geography** — Money Around the World 200

     Map and Globe Skill Use a Map Scale 202

Unit 4 Review Current Events Project 204

Vocabulary Preview
Reading Strategies: Predict/Infer, Monitor/Clarify 210

Lesson 1	Core	**First Americans** 212
	Extend	*Literature* — **The Young Woman and the Thunder Beings** 218
Lesson 2	Core	**Explorers Travel the World** 222
	Extend	*History* — The Magnetic Compass 226
Lesson 3	Core	**Jamestown and Plymouth** 228
	Extend	*Readers' Theater* — The Mayflower Crossing 234

Reading/Thinking Skill Identify Cause and Effect 238

Lesson 4	Core	**People from America's Past** 240
	Extend	*Biography* — Two Patriots 246

Reading/Thinking Skill Compare Fact and Opinion . . . 250

Lesson 5	Core	**Past Heroes** 252
	Extend	*Primary Source* — Learn from a Letter 258
Lesson 6	Core	**Communities Change** 260
	Extend	*Biography* — Inventors in Transportation 264

Citizenship Skill Understand Point of View 266

Lesson 7	Core	**Communication Changes** 268
	Extend	*History* — Runners with a Message 272

Unit 5 Review Current Events Project 274

UNIT 6 | America's Government

278

Vocabulary Preview
Reading Strategies: Summarize, Question 280

Lesson 1
Core | **Government and People** 282
Extend | Literature — **The Fire Station** 288

Lesson 2
Core | **Citizens Make a Difference** 292
Extend | Readers' Theater — Solving Problems 296

Lesson 3
Core | **Laws** 300
Extend | Biography — Rosa Parks 304

 Graph and Chart Skill Read a Pictograph 306

Lesson 4
Core | **Leaders** 308
Extend | Citizenship — Voting with Ballots 312

Citizenship Skill Resolve a Conflict 314

Lesson 5
Core | **National Government** 316
Extend | Citizenship — Democracy 320

Lesson 6
Core | **Our Nation and the World** 322
Extend | Geography — Flags of Different Nations 326

Unit 6 Review Current Events Project 328

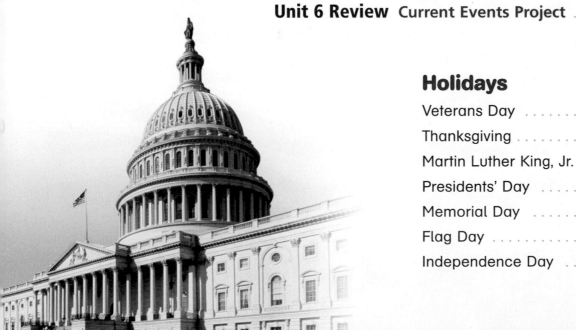

Holidays

Veterans Day 332

Thanksgiving 333

Martin Luther King, Jr. Day 334

Presidents' Day 335

Memorial Day 336

Flag Day 337

Independence Day 338

References

Citizenship Handbook R1

   Our Flag R2

   Songs of Our Nation R4

   Character Traits R8

Resources

Geographic Terms R10

Atlas R12

Picture Glossary R20

Index R36

Primary Source References R46

Credits/Acknowledgments R49

Extend Lessons

Connect the core lesson to an important concept and dig into it. Extend your social studies knowledge!

Literature

"Recess Rules"	30
The Great Smokies	80
"Maple Talk"	106
"The Star-Spangled Banner"	142
The Milkmaid	162
The Young Woman and the Thunder Beings	218
The Fire Station (excerpt)	288

Readers' Theater

Big Storm Coming	88
The Mayflower Crossing	234
Solving Problems	296

Economics

Markets	56
Spend Your Dollar	184

Citizenship

Yo-Yo Ma	132
Voting with Ballots	312
Democracy	320

Primary Sources

Immigrants at Ellis Island	122
Learn from a Letter	258

More primary sources at www.eduplace.com/kids/hmss/

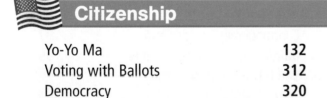

Geography

Languages of Switzerland	96
Money Around the World	200
Flags of Different Nations	326

Biographies

Maggie Cervantes	40
Sally Ride	70
Cesar Chavez	148
Scientists Serving Others	
Marie Curie	
Louis Pasteur	
George Washington Carver	
Eloy Rodriguez	174
Two Patriots	
Abigail Adams and Paul Revere	246
Inventors in Transportation:	
Granville T. Woods and Taylor G. Wang	264
Rosa Parks	304

Education Place®
More biographies at
www.eduplace.com/kids/hmss/

History

A City Grows Taller	48
First Farmers	170
Keeping Food Cold	194
The Magnetic Compass	226
Runners with a Message	272

Skill Lessons

Take a step-by-step approach to learning and practicing key social studies skills.

Map and Globe Skills

Review Maps, Globes, Symbols, Directions	32
Use a Grid	42
Parts of a Globe	72
Use Intermediate Directions	82
Use a Map Scale	202

Chart and Graph Skills

Read a Calendar	50
Read a Timeline	124
Read a Bar Graph	178
Read a Pictograph	306

Study Skills

Conduct an Interview	134
Use Reference Books	186

Citizenship Skills

Make a Decision	150
Understand Point of View	266
Resolve a Conflict	314

Reading and Thinking Skills

Identify Main Idea and Details	98
Compare Fact and Fiction	164
Identify Cause and Effect	238
Compare Fact and Opinion	250

Reading Skills/Graphic Organizer

Compare and Contrast 26, 52, 74, 222, 228

Main Idea and Details 36, 84, 92, 126, 268, 300

Cause and Effect 44, 196

Classify 66, 136, 144, 172, 212, 252, 292, 316

Sequence 100, 188, 240, 260, 308

Draw Conclusions 116, 166, 282

Predict Outcomes 160, 180

Problem and Solution 322

Visual Learning

Maps, graphs, and charts help you learn.

Maps

North Pole, South Pole	32
World Map	33
Santa Rosa	35
Sacramento Neighborhoods	38
Use a Grid	43
San Diego and Spring Valley	47
Brown Elementary School	60
The United States of America	67
North America	68
World Continents	69
Northern, Southern, Western, and Eastern Hemispheres	73
Sierra Nevada	74
Yosemite Valley	75
Florida	76
Nebraska	77
Massachusetts	78
Mississippi River	79
United States	83
Two Cities	86
Landform Regions of the United States	93
Plant Regions of the United States	94
Languages in Switzerland	97
Rainfall in the United States	99
Some Land and Water in North America	108
Parts of a Globe	110
Southwestern States	110
San Francisco, Havre, New York City	118
Where Our Ancestors Came From	120
Landmarks in the United States	138
Mesopotamia	170
Trading Bananas and Wheat	198
Money Around the World	200
Eastern United States	203
Route to Airport	206

Four First American Groups	213
Route from Europe to Asia	223
Christopher Columbus's First Journey, 1492	224
Routes to North America	229
Routes of the Pilgrims, 1620	239
The Thirteen Colonies	241
Lakota Homelands	253
Israel	254
Plainfield, Illinois, in 1873	261
Plainfield, Illinois, Today	261
Inca Lands	272
The United States of America	284
World Leaders Meet	324
Mexico, Japan, Ghana	326
The World: Political	R12
The World: Physical	R14
North America	R16
The United States	R18

Charts and Graphs

Calendar	51
Where People Live	58
Calendar	60
Weather Chart	84
American Culture	152
Sally's Choices	161
Milk Produced Each Year	179
Money in Gina's Savings Account	183
Resources	191
Producers and Consumers	204
Number of Workers in Our School	206
Compare Groups	214
Services	286
How to Solve a Problem	295
Number of Cans Collected	307
Government Leaders	309
A Citizen's Government	328
Votes for Our Field Trip	330

Diagrams

From Tree to Barrel	54
Changing the Environment	103
Jamestown	230
Plymouth	232
Citizens' Responsibilities	294
Geographic Terms	R10

Timelines

Andrea's Family History	124
Dan's Life History	154
Keeping Food Cold	194
Road to Independence	242
Abigail Adams	246
Paul Revere	248
Transportation Changes Plainfield	262
Timeline in American History	274

Fine Art

The Boy, Thomas Hart Benton	129
Totem Pole	129
Mount Rushmore	138
Marco Polo portrait	222
Marco Polo at the Court of Kublai Khan	223
Christopher Columbus portrait	225
Battle of Lexington	242
Washington Crossing the Delaware	244
Benjamin Franklin portrait	245
Samuel Adams portrait	245
Abigail Adams portrait	246
Abigail Adams statue	247
Paul Revere portrait	248
Paul Revere statue	249
Sitting Bull portrait	253
Inca Runners	273
The Constitutional Convention	317

About Your Textbook

❶ How It's Organized

Units The major sections of your book are units.
Each starts with a big idea.

Explore big ideas in geography, history, economics, government, and culture.

Get ready for reading.

Each unit opens with a vocabulary preview.

Four important concepts get you started.

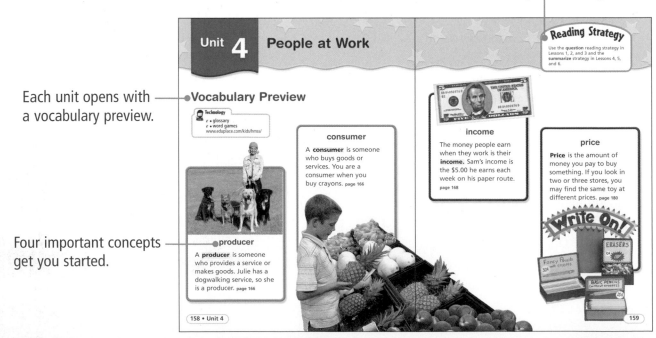

❷ Core and Extend

Lessons The lessons in your book have two parts: core and extend.

Core Lessons
Lessons bring social studies to life and help you meet your state's standards.

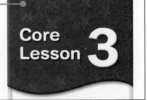

Extend Lessons
Go deeper into an important topic.

Primary Sources

Core Lesson

Vocabulary lists give you the words you need to know.

Reading skills support your understanding of the text.

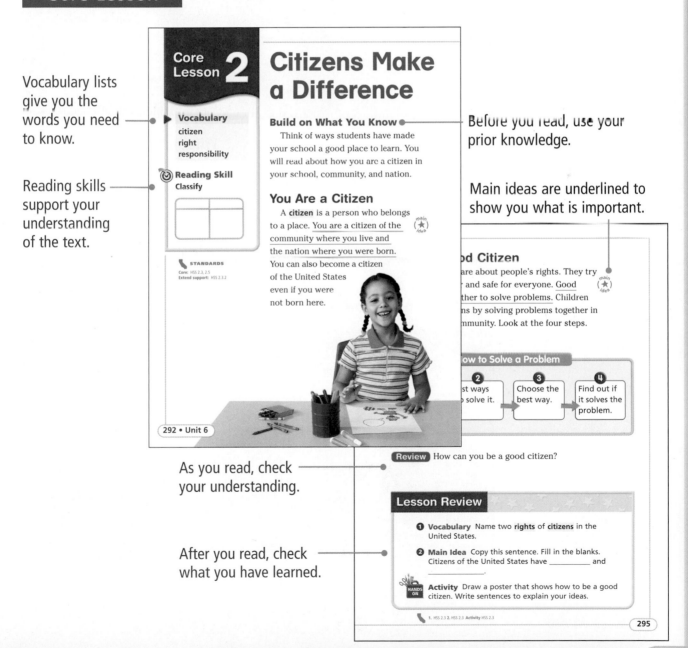

Core Lesson 2

▶ **Vocabulary**
citizen
right
responsibility

🎯 **Reading Skill**
Classify

STANDARDS
Core: HSS 2.3, 2.5
Extend support: HSS 2.3.2

Citizens Make a Difference

Build on What You Know
Think of ways students have made your school a good place to learn. You will read about how you are a citizen in your school, community, and nation.

You Are a Citizen
A **citizen** is a person who belongs to a place. You are a citizen of the community where you live and the nation where you were born. You can also become a citizen of the United States even if you were not born here.

292 • Unit 6

Before you read, use your prior knowledge.

Main ideas are underlined to show you what is important.

...d Citizen
...are about people's rights. They try ...r and safe for everyone. Good ...ther to solve problems. Children ...ns by solving problems together in ...mmunity. Look at the four steps.

...ow to Solve a Problem

❷ ...st ways ...o solve it. → ❸ Choose the best way. → ❹ Find out if it solves the problem.

Review How can you be a good citizen?

Lesson Review

❶ **Vocabulary** Name two **rights** of **citizens** in the United States.

❷ **Main Idea** Copy this sentence. Fill in the blanks. Citizens of the United States have _____ and _____.

HANDS ON Activity Draw a poster that shows how to be a good citizen. Write sentences to explain your ideas.

1. HSS 2.3 2. HSS 2.3 Activity HSS 2.3

295

As you read, check your understanding.

After you read, check what you have learned.

Extend Lesson   Learn more about an important topic from each core lesson.

Dig in and extend your knowledge.

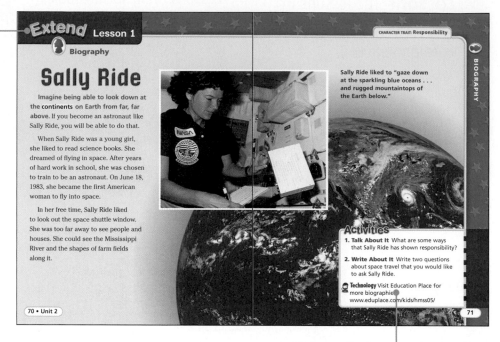

Write, talk, draw, and role-play!

Look for literature, readers' theater, geography, economics—and more.

❸ Skills

Skill Building Learn map, graph, and study skills, as well as citizenship skills for life.

Practice and apply each social studies skill.

Skill lessons step it out.

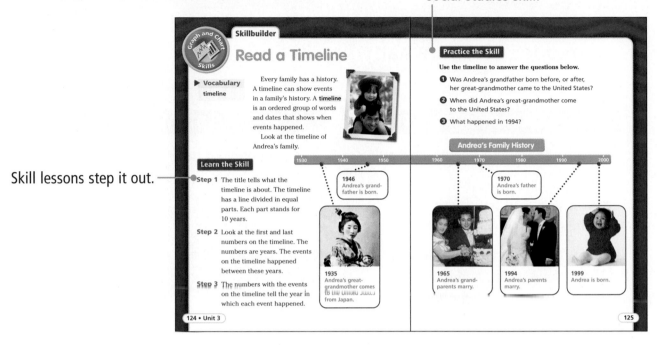

❹ References

Citizenship Handbook

The back of your book includes sections you'll refer to again and again.

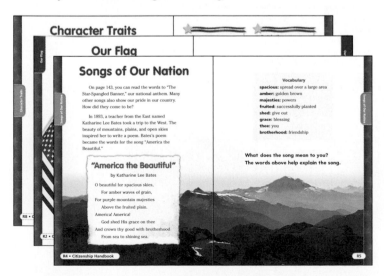

Resources

Look for atlas maps, a glossary of social studies terms, and an index.

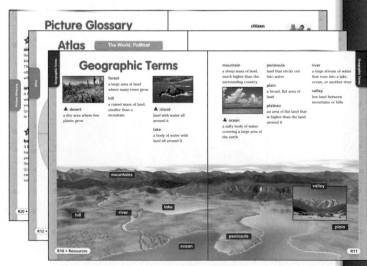

Reading History-Social Science

Your book can help you be a successful reader. Here's what you will find:

VOCABULARY SUPPORT

Preview Learn four important words from the unit.

Lesson Vocabulary Learn the meanings of lesson vocabulary.

Vocabulary Practice Reuse words in the reviews, skills, and extends. Show that you know your vocabulary.

READING STRATEGIES

Look through your book and find the reading strategies at the beginning of each unit.

Predict and Infer

Monitor and Clarify

Question

Summarize

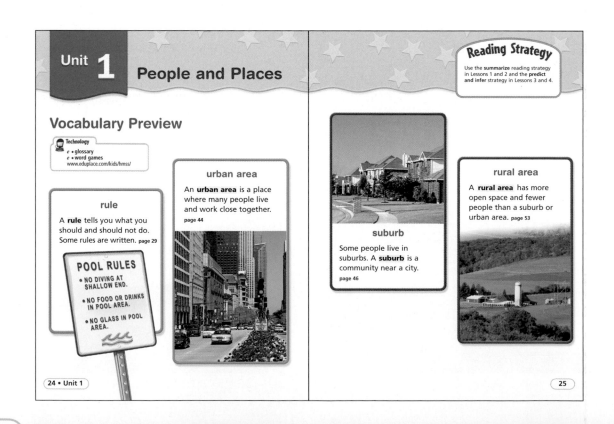

Unit 1 **People and Places**

Reading Strategy
Use the **summarize** reading strategy in Lessons 1 and 2 and the **predict and infer** strategy in Lessons 3 and 4.

Vocabulary Preview

Technology
e • glossary
e • word games
www.eduplace.com/kids/hmss/

rule
A **rule** tells you what you should and should not do. Some rules are written. page 29

POOL RULES
• NO DIVING AT SHALLOW END.
• NO FOOD OR DRINKS IN POOL AREA.
• NO GLASS IN POOL AREA.

urban area
An **urban area** is a place where many people live and work close together. page 44

suburb
Some people live in suburbs. A **suburb** is a community near a city. page 46

rural area
A **rural area** has more open space and fewer people than a suburb or urban area. page 53

24 • Unit 1

25

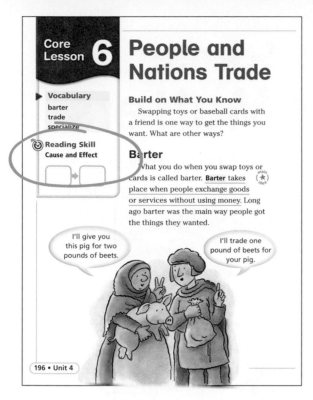

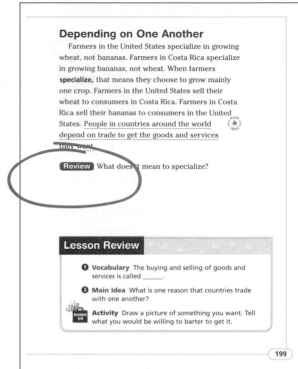

As you read, use the reading skills to organize the information.

Sequence

Cause and Effect

Compare and Contrast

Problem and Solution

Draw Conclusions

Predict Outcomes

Classify

Main Idea and Details

Build on What You Know
Ask yourself what you know about the lesson topic. You may already know a lot!

Review Questions
Answer questions as you read. Did you understand what you read?

Reading

When you come to a word you do not know:

- Look at word parts you may know.

- Think about the sounds for the word parts.

- Say the word parts together.

- Check the word in the sentence to see if the word makes sense.

History-Social Science
Why It Matters

The lessons you read in this book will be exciting and fun. You will use what you learn from the lessons all your life.

WHEN I
- look around my neighborhood
- or read a map—
I'll use geography!

WHEN I
- save money or
- decide what to buy—
I'll use economics!

Town Map

UNIT 1

People and Places

"I live in a city, yes I do
I live in a city, yes I do
I live in a city, yes I do
Made by human hands"

Malvina Reynolds, from the song
"I Live in a City"

The Big Idea

How do land and
people make up
a community?

Vocabulary Preview

Technology

e • **glossary**
e • **word games**
www.eduplace.com/kids/hmss/

rule

A **rule** tells you what you should and should not do. Some rules are written. page 29

POOL RULES

- NO DIVING AT SHALLOW END.
- NO FOOD OR DRINKS IN POOL AREA.
- NO GLASS IN POOL AREA.

urban area

An **urban area** is a place where many people live and work close together. page 44

U-TURNS PERMITTED FOR EMERGENCY VEHICLES ONLY

Reading Strategy

Use the **summarize** reading strategy in Lessons 1 and 2 and the **predict and infer** strategy in Lessons 3 and 4.

suburb

Some people live in suburbs. A **suburb** is a community near a city.

page 46

rural area

A **rural area** has more open space and fewer people than a suburb or urban area. **page 53**

All Kinds of Groups

▶ **Vocabulary**

group
leader
rule

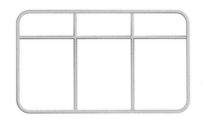

Reading Skill

Compare and Contrast

🔖 **STANDARDS**

Core: HSS 2.5
Extend support: HSS 2.5

Build on What You Know

Do you take a class after school? Are you on a team?

Groups

A **group** is a number of people who live together, work together, or spend time together. You are a part of many groups. Your family is a group. Your school class is a group. The actions of each person in a group make a difference to all.

main
(★)
idea

Charan belongs to these three groups. What other group or groups do you think he might be in?

Review What groups do you belong to?

Family

Class

Afterschool art

Leaders

A **leader** is someone who leads others. The leader of a band helps everyone in the band play music together. Teachers are leaders of their classes. In some classrooms, children take turns being leaders of activities or games. Most groups have leaders.

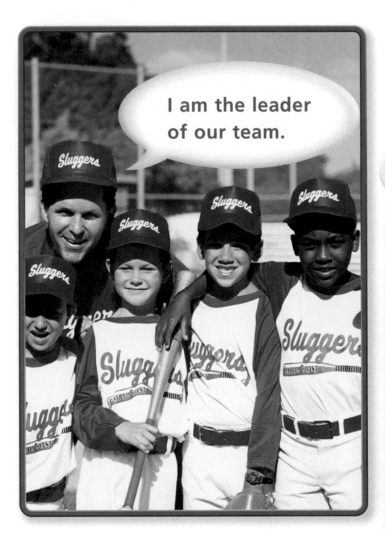

I am the leader of our team.

I follow a leader when I sing.

Rules

A **rule** helps people know what they should and should not do. Most groups have rules. <u>Rules are meant to help people get along.</u> They help people work or play together in the group. Following rules can help the people in a group be safe. In some groups, people talk about their rules. They may make or change their rules together.

main idea

Review Why are rules important in a group?

Some groups have a list of printed rules.

Our Rules
1. Take turns.
2. Talk quietly.
3. Never hurt others.

Lesson Review

❶ **Vocabulary** Give an example of a **rule** for a **group**.

❷ **Main Idea** Give an example of a group that has a leader. Tell how the leader makes a difference.

✏️ **Activity** Write or tell about a group you belong to.

1. HSS 2.5 2. HSS 2.5 **Activity** HSS 2.5

Rules

From the book **Lunch Money and Other Poems About School** by Carol Diggory Shields

Recess Rules

No sliding down the handrails.
No climbing up the slide.
No bouncing on the seesaw.
No throwing sand outside.
No twisting on the swings.
No climbing up the trees.
No jumping from the fences.
No hanging by your knees.

Max slides down the handrails.
He climbs right up the slide.
Max bounces on the seesaw.
He throws the sand outside.
Max twirls the swings up double.
He calls me from a tree.
I climb up. Who gets in trouble?
Max sure doesn't.
Only me.

Activities

1. **Talk About It** Does your school have any recess rules that are not in the poem?

2. **Write About It** Look at the drawing on this page. Write or tell why you think Max does not get in trouble.

31

Review: Maps and Globes

▶ **Vocabulary**

globe
world map

A **globe** is a model of the earth. It shows that the earth is round like a ball. Maps are drawings of places as seen from above. Maps have titles and labels. Some maps have dates.

A **world map** is a flat picture of the earth. You can use a globe and a world map to find continents, oceans, and other places on the earth.

Learn the Skill

Step 1 Find the Atlantic Ocean on the globe and on the world map. In what way is the ocean the same on the map and the globe?

Step 2 Continents are the big bodies of land you see on a globe and a world map. Find North America on the globe and the world map.

Step 3 Globes and maps show countries too. Find Canada on the globe and map.

North Pole

South Pole

Practice the Skill

Look at the globe and the map. Then follow the directions.

1 Compare the globe and the world map. Tell how they are alike and different.

2 Look at the globe and find the continent and country where you live. Then find them on the map. Write their names on a sheet of paper.

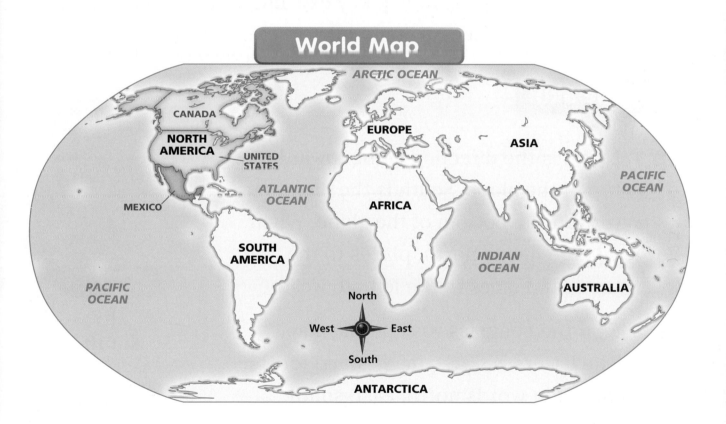

World Map

Skillbuilder

Review: Symbols and Directions

▶ **Vocabulary**

compass rose
symbol

Directions help people find places on globes and maps. A **compass rose** shows cardinal directions. Cardinal directions are north, east, south, and west.

Symbols are pictures that stand for real things. A map key explains what the symbols on a map stand for.

Learn the Skill

Step 1 North is the direction going toward the top of the globe. South is the direction toward the bottom of the globe. When you are facing north, places to the right are east. Places to the left are west.

Step 2 Find the compass rose on the map. The letters N, E, S, and W stand for the direction words north, east, south, and west.

Step 3 Look at the map key, or legend. The symbol for forest is trees. Find the symbol on the map.

North

South

Compass Rose

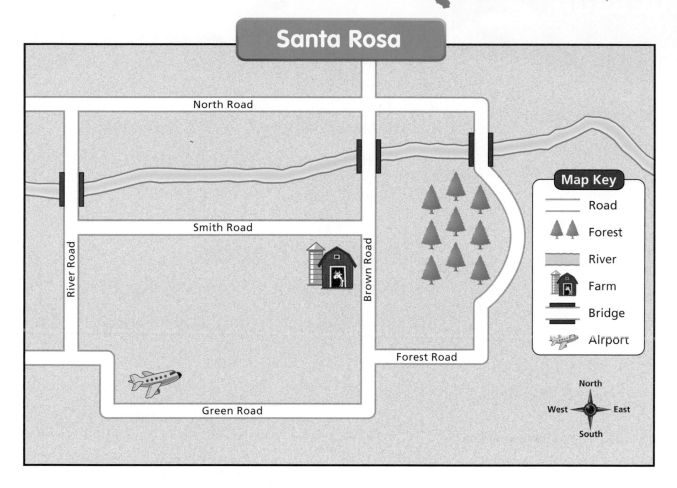

Santa Rosa

Practice the Skill

Look at the map. Then follow the directions.

1 Look at the map key. Describe the symbol for road.

2 Find the roads on the map.

3 Look at the river symbol on the map key. Find the river on the map. What is a symbol that touches the river?

4 Use the compass rose and map key. Name the cardinal directions. What is east of the farm?

Living Together

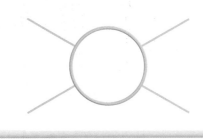
Build on What You Know

Who are some people who live near you? They are your neighbors.

Neighborhoods

You and your neighbors live in a neighborhood. A **neighborhood** is a part of a city or town. Most neighborhoods have homes. Many neighborhoods also have stores, parks, and schools.

main
(★)
idea

Neighborhood Activities

People in a neighborhood do many things together. Children in a neighborhood may play together. They may go to the same school. The grownups may work together to make their neighborhood look better. People may also work together to make their neighborhood safer.

main idea

Review What activities take place in your neighborhood?

What are some places on this map that are in your neighborhood?

Communities

4 A **community** is a place where groups of people live. Cities and towns are communities. A community may have a few or many different neighborhoods.

main (★) idea

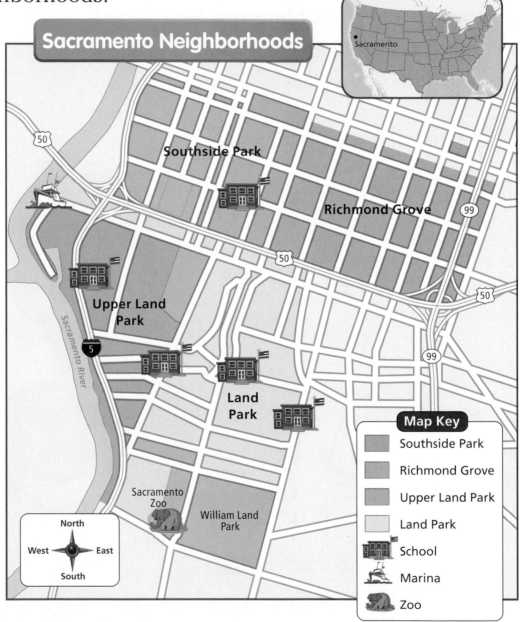

Sacramento Neighborhoods

Southside Park

Richmond Grove

Upper Land Park

Land Park

Sacramento River

Sacramento Zoo

William Land Park

Map Key
- Southside Park
- Richmond Grove
- Upper Land Park
- Land Park
- School
- Marina
- Zoo

North
West — East
South

Skill Reading Maps Name the neighborhoods on this map.

Southside Park, Richmond Grove, Upper Land Park, Land Park

People in a Community

5 People in a community get together for many reasons.

6 Perhaps the community has a fair every year. Often people from different neighborhoods work together to get ready for the event. Others help out on the special day. On Paint Day in Tampa, people work together to help others paint their homes.

Review What are some reasons people get together in communities?

Getting ready for fair, helping out on the day of fair, painting houses

Paint Your Heart Out
TAMPA

Lesson Review

❶ Vocabulary Explain what a **community** is.

❷ Main Idea What are some ways people work together in neighborhoods and communities?

Activity Think about the places you go in your neighborhood. Then draw a picture map that shows those places.

1. Analysis Skill HI 2 **2.** Analysis Skill HI 2 **Activity** HSS 2.2

Biography

Maggie Cervantes

Maggie Cervantes (suhr VAHN tays) is a **community** leader in the city of Los Angeles, California. She makes sure that neighbors of all ages meet and help each other. As a child, Cervantes saw that many of her neighbors needed jobs. Some needed better places to live. Cervantes promised herself that some day she would help her community.

Maggie Cervantes as a baby

Maggie Cervantes kept her promise. Today she leads a group that helps people in Los Angeles. Her group helped build safe housing for women and their children. In the buildings are child care centers and places where women learn job skills.

Cervantes says that most of all she loves "bringing people together to get a project done."

Activities

1. **Talk About It** Why did Maggie Cervantes want to help the people in her community?

2. **Write About It** Write or tell two questions you would ask Maggie Cervantes if she visited your class.

 Technology Visit Education Place for more biographies. www.eduplace.com/kids/hmss/

Use a Grid

Grids can help you find **locations**, or places on maps. A **grid** is a pattern of lines that make columns and rows. Each column has a letter, and each row has a number. The letters and the numbers name each square.

▶ **Vocabulary**

location
grid

Learn the Skill

Step 1 Look at this grid. Put your finger on the star. Move it straight up to the top of the column. What is the letter?

Step 2 Put your finger on the star again. Move it sideways to the beginning of the row. What is the number?

Step 3 Together, the letter and number name the square B3. That is the exact point, or absolute location, where the star can be found. The absolute location on a grid tells you the exact place where something is. A map or grid can also show relative location, the place where something is in relation to something else. The star is near the diamond.

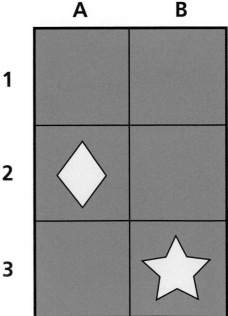

Practice the Skill

Look at the map. Then answer the questions.

1 Where is the absolute location of the library?

2 Give the relative location of the post office to the library.

3 What is located in square D4?

4 Make a grid map of your classroom.

43

Cities and Suburbs

Vocabulary

urban area
suburb

**Reading Skill**

Cause and Effect

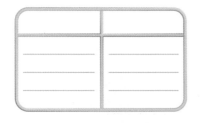

STANDARDS

Core: HSS 2.2.4, Analysis Skill HI 2
Extend support: HSS 2.1, Analysis Skill CST 3,
Analysis Skill HI 2

Build on What You Know

Maybe you live in a community that has houses with big yards. Or do you live where buildings are close together?

Cities

A city is a place where many people live and work. Cars, trucks, and buses fill the streets. In some urban areas, tall buildings rise into the sky. **Urban area** is another name for city. Buildings are close together in cities. There may be little space for grassy yards. Children play in city parks. **1**

Skill **Reading Visuals** Compare business centers in two urban areas.

Cities Are Different

main idea

<u>Not all cities are alike.</u> Not even all parts of one city are alike. Often one part of a city has many office buildings close together. Another part of the city may have a zoo, a river, a park, or smaller buildings that are farther apart.

Review What things can you see in urban areas?

45

Suburbs

Some people live in suburbs. A **suburb** is a community near a city. Spring Valley is a suburb of San Diego.

main idea ⭐

Spring Valley has many homes like this one.

Spring Valley also has apartments and homes like these.

Spring Valley is a big suburb. It has a large amount of land and a large number of people too. In some ways, Spring Valley is like a city. With so many people, Spring Valley needs 18 schools. It has many grocery stores, pizza shops, and other businesses.

Suburbs Depend on Cities

Usually a city has more places to work and shop than any of its suburbs has. Many people who live in suburbs depend on the nearby city for jobs. Also, people come to have fun in a city. People from suburbs all around San Diego can visit the famous San Diego Zoo. Visitors also like Old Town. It shows the way San Diego looked long ago.

main idea (★)

Skill **Reading Maps** Find Spring Valley and San Diego. What other suburbs do you see?

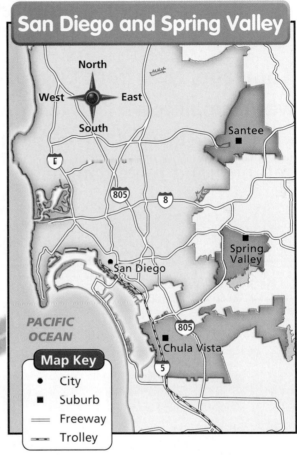

San Diego and Spring Valley

North
West   East
South

Santee

805   8

Spring Valley

San Diego

PACIFIC OCEAN

Chula Vista

805

5

Map Key
- • City
- ■ Suburb
- — Freeway
- ═ Trolley

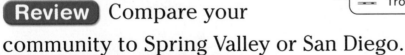

Review Compare your community to Spring Valley or San Diego.

Lesson Review

1 **Vocabulary** Write a sentence that tells two ways that an **urban area** is different from a **suburb.**

2 **Main Idea** What is one way that a suburb depends on a city?

HANDS ON

Activity Draw a picture map that shows your community and the nearest city or suburb.

1. HSS 2.2.4 2. HSS 2.2.4 **Activity** HSS 2.2

A City Grows Taller

Long ago, New York City was not a city at all. It was a small town. Not far from the center of town, people farmed the land. They grew vegetables and raised animals.

New York once looked like this.

Over the years, more and more people moved to New York. It became a city. In time, the city had a problem. It started to run out of open space.

To solve their problem, New Yorkers began to build skyscrapers. These tall buildings could hold many people and businesses. They used little land space. Today New York City has more than eight million people and many skyscrapers.

Activities

1. **Talk About It** Why did New York City grow taller?

2. **Look Into It** Compare how people used land in each picture.

Read a Calendar

▶ **Vocabulary**

calendar

Cities and suburbs have community events. A calendar can help citizens keep track of the events. A **calendar** is a way of showing time. A calendar shows months, weeks, and days.

Learn the Skill

Step 1 Name the months of the year in order. Start with January. Then look at the calendar page at right. What month does it show?

Step 2 Each row on the calendar shows one week. Name the seven days of the week. Start with Sunday.

Step 3 Every day of the month has a number, or date. Find the square with the number 6. The date of that day is November 6.

Step 4 Find the community event on the first Saturday of the month. What is it?

Practice the Skill

Look at this community calendar page.
Then answer the questions.

1 What holiday is on November 11?

2 What day of the week is Thanksgiving?

NOVEMBER

Sunday	Monday	Tuesday	Wednesday	Thursday	Friday	Saturday
			1	2	3	4 Fall Fair
5	6	7 ✓ Election Day	8	9	10	11 Veterans Day
12	13	14	15	16	17	18
19	20	21	22	23 Thanksgiving	24	25
26	27	28	29	30		

Rural Communities

Vocabulary

rural area
market

Reading Skill

Compare and Contrast

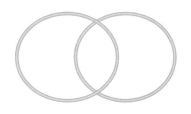

STANDARDS

Core: HSS 2.2.4, Analysis Skill HI 2
Extend support: HSS 2.4

Build on What You Know

Do you live on a farm or in a small town? In some ways, your community is different from a city or a suburb.

Small Towns

Outside of cities and suburbs are rural areas. People in rural areas may live in small towns. Small towns have fewer stores, schools, and homes than cities or suburbs have.

Farms

Rural areas are places with more open space than cities and suburbs. That is why most farms are in rural areas. Farmers need a lot of space to raise animals or crops, such as fruit and vegetables.

The vegetables that you eat may come from farms like this one in California.

Review Why don't you find farms in cities?

Forests

The wood people use for buildings, chairs, and other things comes from trees. Trees grow in forests. <u>Most forests are found in rural areas because trees need space to grow.</u>

(main idea ★)

❶ Lumber companies have workers that cut down trees and saw them into logs.

❷ Logs go to a sawmill to be cut into boards.

❸ Barrels are an example of something that might be made from wood.

Review What are some ways that land is used in rural areas?

Markets

Forest workers and farmers sell their wood and the things they grow. They send those things to markets. A **market** can be anywhere people buy and sell things. People in rural areas may send things they make or grow to markets in cities and suburbs.

Food grown in rural areas is sold in city markets.

Lesson Review

❶ **Vocabulary** Describe a **rural area** in one or two sentences.

❷ **Main Idea** What are two ways that rural areas are different from urban areas?

✏ **Activity** Describe ways people use land in your community. Compare different land use in a city, suburb, or rural area in California.

1. HSS 2.2.4 2. HSS 2.2.4 **Activity** HSS 2.2.4, Analysis Skill HI 2

Economics

Markets

Are you buying? Are you selling? You are in a **market.** In smaller markets, people buy the things they want for their own use. In large markets, businesses buy materials they need to make things. For example, you might have a business that makes chairs. You would go to a big market where many kinds of wood are sold.

People can buy many different things on an Internet marketplace.

This man sells spices in an open market in Marrakesh, Morocco.

Market

A supermarket is filled with many kinds of foods and other things.

Fishers send their catch to markets like this one in Japan. Here business owners buy large amounts of fish.

Activities

1. **Make It** Make a poster showing the names and prices of some things you would find in a market.

2. **Write About It** Write or tell the kinds of things you would sell if you owned a market.

Where People Live

Rural Area

Suburb

Urban Area

Choose the missing words that help describe the chart.

An **1.** _____ has the most buildings and people.
A **2.** _____ is close to a city. A **3.** _____ has the fewest buildings and people.

STANDARDS **1.** HSS 2.2.4 **2.** HSS 2.2.4 **3.** HSS 2.2.4

Facts and Main Ideas

4. What can leaders do to help a group? (page 28)

5. Why are rules important to a group? (page 29)

6. Why are markets important to people in rural and urban areas? (page 55)

7. What is one way that people can help a community? (pages 37, 39)

4. HSS 2.5 **5.** HSS 2.3.1 **6.** HSS 2.2.4 **7.** HSS 2.5

Choose the letter of the correct word.

8. A person who leads others

9. Anywhere people buy and sell things

10. Something that tells what people should or should not do

11. A number of people who work, live, or spend time together

12. A place where a group of people live, work, and follow the same rules and laws

A. **market** (page 55)

B. **rule** (page 29)

C. **community** (page 38)

D. **group** (page 26)

E. **leader** (page 28)

8. HSS 2.5 9. HSS 2.2.4 10. HSS 2.3.1 11. HSS 2.2.4 12. HSS 2.2.4
13. HSS 2.2.4

 Test Practice

13. What does the word **neighborhood** mean?

   A. a person who leads others

   B. a part of a city or town

   C. anywhere that people buy and sell things

   D. something that tells people what to do

Critical Thinking

Compare and Contrast

14. What are some ways that a suburb is the same as a rural area?

14. HSS 2.2.4

Review

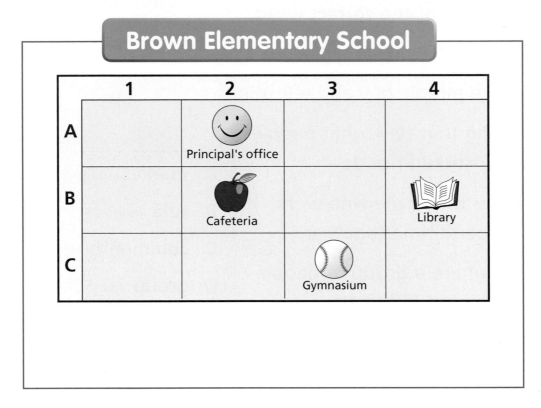

Brown Elementary School

	1	2	3	4
A		Principal's office		
B		Cafeteria		Library
C			Gymnasium	

15. What is the absolute location of the cafeteria? Name the square.

16. Which room is in square 4B?

15. HSS 2.2.1 16. HSS 2.2

Read a Calendar

17. Which holiday is on October 23?

18. What is the date of Columbus Day?

17. Analysis Skill CST 1 18. Analysis Skill CST 1

Unit Activity

The Big Idea

Give a Short Report

Choose a lesson you have read. Make note cards to help you tell about the lesson. Then plan a short report on the land and the people you read about.

1 On one card, write something you learned in the lesson.

2 On another card, write or draw something you liked about the lesson.

Our Town is a suburb of San Diego.

Current Events

Find out what leaders in your community are doing. Make a **Leaders in the News Chart.**

LEADER'S NAME	JOB	PLACE

Technology

Read articles about current events at **www.eduplace.com/kids/hmss/**

In Your Classroom

Look for these Social Studies Independent Books in your classroom.

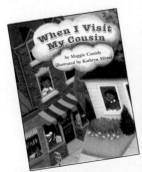

When I Visit My Cousin
by Maggie Cassidy
Illustrated by Kathryn Mitter

Jaime Escalante a Great Teacher
by Carol Peske

Cherry Blossoms Everywhere

At the Library

You may find these books at your school or public library.

On the Town: A Community Adventure
by Judith Caseley

School Rules
by Larry Dane Brimmer

UNIT 2

Places Near and Far

"All I could see from
where I stood
Was three long mountains
and a wood;
I turned and looked
another way,
And saw three islands
in a bay."

Edna St. Vincent Millay,
from the poem "Renascence"

The Big Idea

Why is the world
around you important
in your life?

Vocabulary Preview

Technology

e • **glossary**
e • **word games**
www.eduplace.com/kids/hmss/

landform

A **landform** is one of the shapes of land found on the earth. One kind of landform is a plain. **page 74**

continent

The United States is on the continent of North America. A **continent** is a large body of land. **page 68**

Reading Strategy

Use the **question** reading strategy in Lessons 1, 2, and 3 and the **monitor and clarify** strategy in Lessons 4 and 5.

climate

Climate is the usual weather of a place over a long time. People in a cold climate need warm homes to live in. **page 85**

natural resource

Water is an important natural resource. A **natural resource** is something in nature that people use. **page 100**

Your Address

Build on What You Know

What do you call the community where you live? Do you know the rest of your address?

Vocabulary

country
state
continent
nation

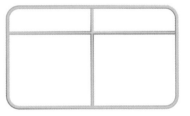

Reading Skill
Classify

STANDARDS

Core: HSS 2.2, 2.2.2, Analysis Skill HI 2
Extend support: HSS 2.5

States in a Country

Carlos is going to mail a letter to his cousin Len. Len lives on Green Street in the city of Columbus. Look at the envelope to see the rest of the address. What is Ohio? What does U.S.A. mean?

return address

stamp

address

Carlos Rivera
95 Rock Street
Toronto, Ontario
Canada
M6C 2J9

Len Ruis
27 Green Street
Columbus, Ohio 430
U.S.A.

Carlos

The United States of America

ALASKA

CANADA

North
West · East
South

WASHINGTON
OREGON
IDAHO
MONTANA
NORTH DAKOTA
MINNESOTA
WISCONSIN
MICHIGAN
SOUTH DAKOTA
WYOMING
NEBRASKA
IOWA
ILLINOIS
INDIANA
OHIO
NEW YORK
PENNSYLVANIA
NEVADA
UTAH
COLORADO
KANSAS
MISSOURI
WEST VIRGINIA
VIRGINIA
CALIFORNIA
ARIZONA
NEW MEXICO
OKLAHOMA
ARKANSAS
TENNESSEE
NORTH CAROLINA
SOUTH CAROLINA
MISSISSIPPI
ALABAMA
GEORGIA
TEXAS
LOUISIANA
FLORIDA

NEW HAMPSHIRE
VERMONT
MASSACHUSETTS
MAINE
RHODE ISLAND
CONNECTICUT
NEW JERSEY
DELAWARE
MARYLAND

Toronto

Columbus

PACIFIC OCEAN

ATLANTIC OCEAN

HAWAII

MEXICO

Gulf of Mexico

Map Key
· City

The city of Columbus is in the state of Ohio.

The letters U.S.A. on the envelope stand for the country called the United States of America. A **country** is a land where people have the same laws and leaders. Ohio is a state in the United States. A **state** is a part of a country. The United States is a country made up of 50 states.

Len

main
(★)
idea

Review Which state do you live in?

67

Continents

If you were an astronaut looking at the earth from a space station, you would see mostly oceans. You would also see some very large bodies of land. Most of those large bodies of land are **continents**.  Look at the continent of North America on the map below and on pages R16 and R17.

The United States is on the continent of North America. The United States shares North America with two other large countries, or nations, Canada and Mexico. **Nation** is another word for country.

North America

Skill **Reading Maps** Seven small nations and many island countries are part of North America too. Which direction is Mexico from the United States?

Reading Maps Find and name the seven continents on the map. Find and name the four oceans.

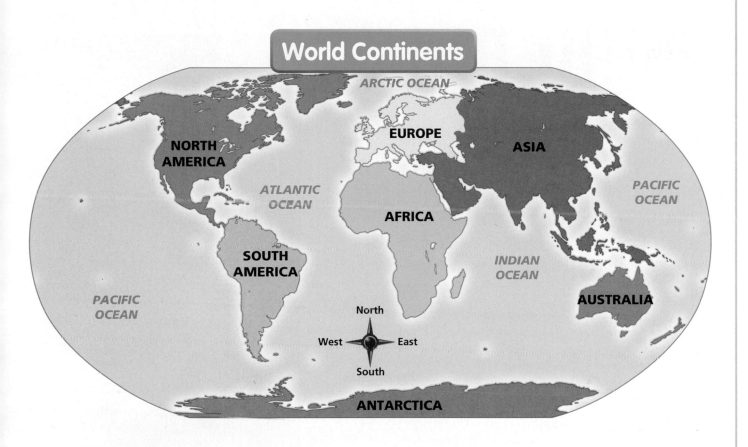

World Continents

ARCTIC OCEAN

EUROPE

ASIA

NORTH AMERICA

ATLANTIC OCEAN

PACIFIC OCEAN

AFRICA

SOUTH AMERICA

INDIAN OCEAN

PACIFIC OCEAN

AUSTRALIA

North

West — East

South

ANTARCTICA

Review What is one way that Mexico and the United States are alike?

Lesson Review

❶ **Vocabulary** Write a sentence that tells where you live. Use the words **country**, **state**, and **continent** in the sentence.

❷ **Main Idea** What are the earth's seven continents?

Activity Draw an envelope for a letter to a friend. Write your address and your friend's address on it.

Sally Ride

Imagine being able to look down at the **continents** on Earth from far, far above. If you become an astronaut like Sally Ride, you will be able to do that.

When Sally Ride was a young girl, she liked to read science books. She dreamed of flying in space. After years of hard work in school, she was chosen to train to be an astronaut. On June 18, 1983, she became the first American woman to fly into space.

In her free time, Sally Ride liked to look out the space shuttle window. She was too far away to see people and houses. She could see the Mississippi River and the shapes of farm fields along it.

Sally Ride liked to "gaze down at the sparkling blue oceans . . . and rugged mountaintops of the Earth below."

Activities

1. **Talk About It** What are some ways that Sally Ride has shown responsibility?

2. **Write About It** Write two questions about space travel that you would like to ask Sally Ride.

Technology Visit Education Place for more biographies. www.eduplace.com/kids/hmss/

Skillbuilder

Parts of a Globe

▶ **Vocabulary**

pole
equator
hemisphere

To show locations on a globe, we use the **poles,** the **equator,** and **hemispheres.**

Learn the Skill

Step 1 The equator is an imaginary line around the middle of the earth. Where is the equator on the globe?

Step 2 The equator divides the earth into the Northern Hemisphere and the Southern Hemisphere.

Step 3 The maps on page 73 show that the earth may also be divided into Eastern and Western hemispheres. Compare the photograph of Earth to the globe. In what ways are they the same?

North Pole

South Pole

Practice the Skill

Look at the maps. Then follow the directions.

1 Find the continent where you live. Tell which hemispheres you live in.

2 Which continent has land in all four hemispheres?

3 Name two continents in the Southern Hemisphere.

Northern Hemisphere

Southern Hemisphere

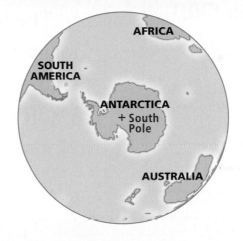

Western Hemisphere

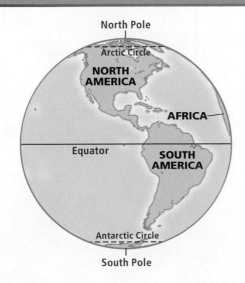

Eastern Hemisphere

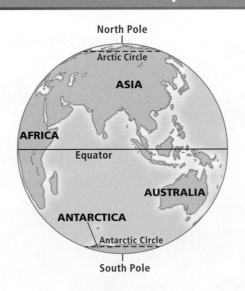

Core Lesson 2

Land and Water

Vocabulary

landform
valley
island
peninsula
lake

Reading Skill

Compare and Contrast

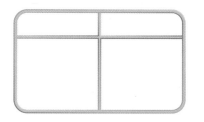

Build on What You Know

Think about your community. Is it flat? Is it hilly? Is there a body of water nearby?

Landforms

The land on the earth is shaped in many different ways. Each different shape, such as a hill or mountain, is a **landform.** The pictures on pages 74 to 77 show some different landforms.

STANDARDS

Core: Analysis Skill HI 2
Extend support: Analysis Skill HI 2

Sierra Nevada in California

mountains

Yosemite Valley in California

A **valley** is low land between mountains or hills. Often a valley has been carved out by a river running through it. More people choose to farm in valleys than on the steep sides of mountains.

Review Why do you think people are more likely to farm in valleys than in mountains?

A peninsula and an island in Rhode Island

Islands and peninsulas are a little alike. An **island** is land with water all around it. A **peninsula** is land that has water on three sides. Most of the state of Florida is a peninsula. The Delmarva Peninsula has all of Delaware and parts of Maryland and Virginia.

plain

A plain in Nebraska

A plain is mostly flat land. Most of the middle of the United States is covered by plains. Other plains are found on the land along the Atlantic Ocean and the Gulf of Mexico.

Review What is one landform in California?

Water

Water comes in many shapes and forms too. You have read that most of the earth is covered with ocean water. Ocean water is salty. Most bodies of water found on land have fresh water.

A lake in Massachusetts

A **lake** is a body of water with land all around it. Most lakes have fresh water. Lakes come in many sizes. Some are small mountain lakes. Others, like Lake Superior, are huge. Find Lake Superior and the other four Great Lakes on a map of the United States.

river

The Mississippi River

A river is a long, moving body of fresh water. Rivers flow downhill into oceans, lakes, or other rivers. Find the Mississippi River and the Missouri River on the map on page 83.

Review What is a difference between an ocean and most lakes?

Lesson Review

1 **Vocabulary** Write one or two sentences that tell what you know about **landforms.**

2 **Main Idea** What are some kinds of land and water on the earth?

Activity Draw a picture of how people use land and water in your community.

1. HI 2   2. HI 2   **Activity** HI 2

The Great Smokies

A legend is a story that is told and retold over many, many years. Joseph Bruchac retold this Cherokee legend for the book **Between Earth & Sky**. It tells about **landforms.**

If we should travel
far to the South,
there in the land
of mountains and mist,
we might hear the story
of how Earth was first shaped.

Water Beetle came out
to see if it was ready,
but the ground was
still as wet as a swamp,
too soft for anyone to stand.

Great Buzzard said, "I will help dry the land."
He began to fly close above the new Earth.
Where his wings came down,
valleys were formed,
and where his wings lifted,
hills rose up through the mist.

So the many rolling valleys and hills
of that place called the Great Smokies
came into being there.

Activities

1. **Talk About It** How does the Cherokee legend say that valleys were formed?

2. **Draw It** Make a U.S. map showing the Appalachian Mountains and the Great Smokies.

Use Intermediate Directions

▶ **Vocabulary**

northeast
southeast
southwest
northwest

When people travel from one city to another, they often use maps to find their way. A compass rose shows them the directions.

Learn the Skill

Look at the compass rose below.

Step 1 Point to the directions north, south, east, and west. The letters N, S, E, and W stand for each direction word.

Step 2 Find the line halfway between north and east. This line points in the direction called **northeast.**

Step 3 Now find the line halfway between south and west. This line points in the direction called **southwest.**

Step 4 Find the letters NE, SE, SW, and NW. These letters stand for the intermediate direction words **northeast, southeast, southwest,** and **northwest.**

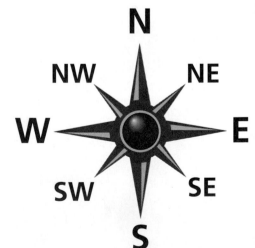

Practice the Skill

Look at the map. Then follow the directions.

1 Find the Great Lakes. In what direction are the Appalachian Mountains from the Great Lakes?

2 Find the Colorado River. What direction would you travel from the Gulf of Mexico to get to the Colorado River?

3 Find the title, legend, and compass rose. Which one shows direction?

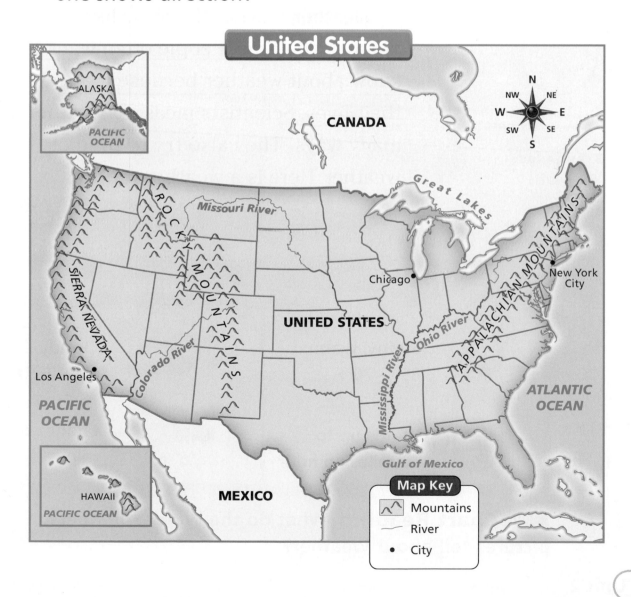

United States

Weather and Climate

Vocabulary
weather
climate

Reading Skill
Main Idea and Details

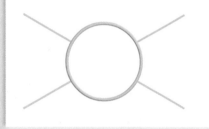

STANDARDS
Core: Analysis Skill HI 2
Extend support: Analysis Skill HI 2

Build on What You Know

Is it raining, snowing, or sunny today? What it is like outside makes a difference in the activities you do each day.

Weather

Weather is what the air is like outside at any given time. People often want to know about weather because it affects their lives. Scientists measure weather in many ways. They also try to predict weather. Here is a weather report.

Today		Tomorrow	
☀	Sunny, warm 65° – 70°F	⛅	Cloudy 60° – 62°F
🌀	Winds up to 10 miles an hour	🌧	Chance of rain

Skill **Chart Reading** What do the words, numbers, and pictures tell about weather?

Climate

Climate is the usual weather of a place over a long time. A climate can have different kinds of weather. Jim and Jenna tell about the climate where they live.

July can be very hot in Milwaukee, Wisconsin.

Jim

January can be really cold.

Jim

Mobile, Alabama, has warm weather most of the year.

Jenna

Rain storms are part of our climate too.

Jenna

Review What are two kinds of weather that could be in one climate?

Living in Different Climates

Climates make a difference in the way people live. *main idea*

In what ways are these two climates different?

Two Cities

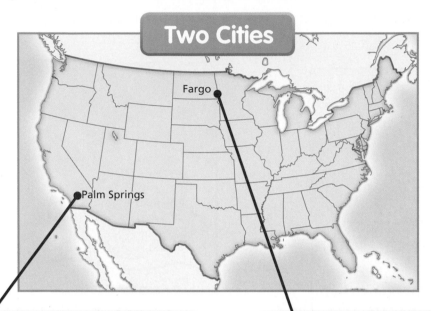

Fargo

Palm Springs

Palm Springs, California

has a climate that is hot and dry in daytime.

People need:
- cool air in buildings and cars year round
- light clothes to wear

Fargo, North Dakota

has a climate that is very cold in winter.

People need:
- warm air in buildings and cars in winter
- clothes to keep out snow and cold

Cold Climate Job

How do you know that this picture was not taken in Palm Springs?

Farmers in some parts of California grow oranges. Orange trees do well in California's warm climate. Builders think of climate when they plan homes and other buildings. Also, some jobs fit one climate and not another. Driving a snowplow is one example. In what state would a snowplow driver live?

Review What is one way that climate makes a difference in what people do?

Lesson Review

1 **Vocabulary** Write sentences to explain the difference between **weather** and **climate.**

2 **Main Idea** Explain how weather and climate are related.

Activity Draw a picture that shows how climate affects people where you live. Explain your drawing.

1. Analysis Skill HI 2 2. Analysis Skill HI 2 **Activity** Analysis Skill HI 2

Big Storm Coming

The Gale family lives in a cold climate.
See how a weather prediction helps them.

CAST

Grandmom	**Dean:** age 10
Mom	**Carol Reed:** weather forecaster
Dad	**Narrator**
Annie: age 7	**Chorus:** blizzard sounds

Scene 1

Narrator: It's a cold Monday night in February. The Gale family is at home watching Carol Reed's weather report on TV.

Carol Reed: We've got a big blizzard headed our way tonight, folks. Strong winds will bring us more than twenty inches of snow. Get ready!

Annie: How can we get ready for the blizzard?

Dad: I'll get out the snow shovels. Then I'm going to the store to get batteries, candles, milk, and bread.

Grandmom: Let's cook now in case we lose electricity.

Mom: I'll fill up some water bottles and start a fire in the fireplace.

Dean: I'll charge the phone and check the radio batteries.

Annie: I'll bring in more logs, too.

Narrator: Four hours later, the family watches the latest weather report.

Carol Reed: Blizzard winds are up to 50 miles per hour. Driving is very dangerous. The airport is closed.

Chorus: (howling wind sounds)

Scene 2

Narrator: The family is watching the weather report on Wednesday afternoon.

Carol Reed: We now have 33 inches of snow. This is the worst blizzard in ten years!

Dad: I'm glad we got our supplies ready.

Grandmom: Yes! The electricity was out for nine hours.

Annie: Toasting marshmallows in the fireplace was fun!

Grandmom: Once when I was a girl, I was stuck at school overnight. A big storm surprised us, and no one could travel. People couldn't predict the weather very well then.

Dad: Predictions are much better today.

Mom: Carol Reed predicted this one right.

Dean: I predict we'll dig lots of snow tomorrow.

Annie: Let's make a whole bunch of snow people, too! I wonder if school's going to be closed again?

Carol Reed: The snow should stop late tonight, but most schools will be closed tomorrow. Check the list on your screen.

Annie: Look! Our school's on the list!

Carol Reed: See you tonight at six!

Chorus: (howling wind sounds)

Activities

1. **Talk About It** Tell ways that weather prediction helps people.

2. **Write About It** Write or tell about a storm that you know about. Tell what people did to stay safe.

Regions

Vocabulary

region

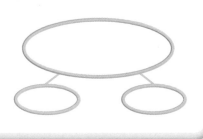
Reading Skill
Main Idea and Details

STANDARDS
Core: HSS 2.2, Analysis Skill HI 2
Extend support: Analysis Skill HI 2

Build on What You Know

Think about your neighborhood. What makes it different from a nearby neighborhood?

Regions

A **region** is an area that has some shared natural or human feature. People use regions as a way of describing places. Some regions are natural regions such as climate, landform, or plant regions. Other regions are human regions. They are described by human features. The languages that people speak and the work they do are two human features.

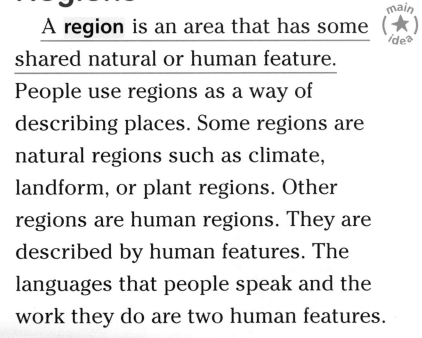

Mountains

Highlands

Landform Regions

Areas with shared landforms are landform regions. The United States has many landform regions. The map shows the main ones.

Review What is one landform region that your state has?

Skill **Reading Maps** Are there more mountains in the southeast or northwest United States?

Landform Regions of the United States

ALASKA
PACIFIC OCEAN

CANADA

N
NW   NE
W   E
SW   SE
S

UNITED STATES

PACIFIC OCEAN

ATLANTIC OCEAN

HAWAII
PACIFIC OCEAN

MEXICO

Gulf of Mexico

Map Key

Plains	Mountains
Great Plains	River
Highlands	Water

Plains

Water

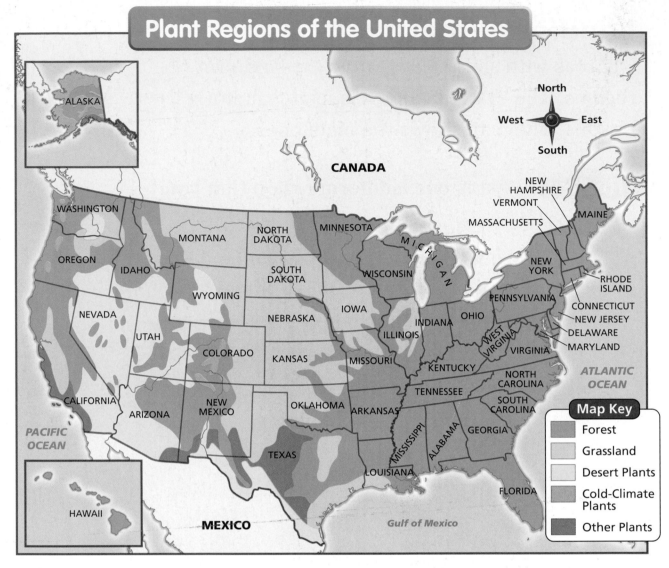

Plant Regions of the United States

North
West — East
South

CANADA

Map Key
- Forest
- Grassland
- Desert Plants
- Cold-Climate Plants
- Other Plants

ALASKA

WASHINGTON
OREGON
IDAHO
MONTANA
NORTH DAKOTA
SOUTH DAKOTA
WYOMING
NEVADA
UTAH
COLORADO
NEBRASKA
KANSAS
CALIFORNIA
ARIZONA
NEW MEXICO
OKLAHOMA
TEXAS
MINNESOTA
IOWA
MISSOURI
ARKANSAS
LOUISIANA
WISCONSIN
MICHIGAN
ILLINOIS
INDIANA
OHIO
KENTUCKY
TENNESSEE
MISSISSIPPI
ALABAMA
GEORGIA
NEW HAMPSHIRE
VERMONT
MAINE
MASSACHUSETTS
NEW YORK
RHODE ISLAND
PENNSYLVANIA
CONNECTICUT
NEW JERSEY
WEST VIRGINIA
DELAWARE
VIRGINIA
MARYLAND
NORTH CAROLINA
SOUTH CAROLINA
FLORIDA

PACIFIC OCEAN

HAWAII

MEXICO

Gulf of Mexico

ATLANTIC OCEAN

Which states have desert plants?

Prickly pear cactus, a desert plant

Plant Regions

main ★ idea

Places may be regions because they have the same kinds of plants growing naturally. The United States has large forest regions and grassland regions. It also has places where few kinds of plants grow. Some places are too dry for most plants. Other places are too cold and windy.

New England

Hawaii

The United States has many kinds of forests. The forest on the left has the kinds of trees that grow in the hot climate of Hawaii. The forest on the right has the kinds of trees that grow in New England's cool climate.

Review What are two kinds of plant regions?

Lesson Review

1 **Vocabulary** Describe one kind of landform **region.**

2 **Main Idea** What region do you live in?

 Activity Use the map on page 94. Draw a picture of the kinds of plants that grow naturally in your region.

1. Analysis Skill HI 2 2. Analysis Skill HI 2 **Activity** Analysis Skill HI 2

Languages of Switzerland

One day Marie visited a city in Switzerland called Genf. At the same time, her friend Sam visited Genève, and her friend Kim went to Ginevra. Surprise! They all met in the same city! How can a city have more than one name?

Switzerland is a small country, but it has many regions and four national languages. In the past, people in each **region** spoke a different language. Today, the regions are not as clear. Most people in Switzerland speak more than one language. Still, many signs say the same thing in three or four languages.

SWITZERLAND

Languages in Switzerland

Map Key
- German
- French
- Italian
- Romansh

GERMANY

Basel

Zürich

FRANCE

Bern

AUSTRIA

Lausanne

Geneva

North

West — East

South

ITALY

Skill **Reading Maps** Which language is spoken in most of Switzerland?

Activities

1. **Read a Map** Which is the second largest language region in Switzerland?

2. **Write About It** Explain how Marie, Sam, and Kim could go to Genf, Genève, and Ginevra and still be in the same city.

Reading and Thinking Skills

Skillbuilder

Identify Main Idea and Details

▶ **Vocabulary**

main idea
detail

Knowing about main ideas and details can help you understand what you read.

Learn the Skill

Look for the **main idea** and **details** in this paragraph.

Live oak leaves and acorns

Different kinds of trees grow in different regions of the United States. Honey mesquite (meh SKEET) trees grow where it is hot and dry. White spruce trees grow where it is cold in winter. Live oak trees grow in warm, wet regions.

main ★ idea

Step 1 The main idea tells what the whole paragraph is about. In this paragraph, the first sentence tells the main idea. But the main idea can be any sentence that tells what the whole paragraph is about.

Step 2 The other sentences in this paragraph give the details. Each detail tells more about the main idea.

Practice the Skill

Read the paragraph below and look at the map.

1 Tell the main idea of this paragraph.

2 Give one detail from the paragraph and one detail from the map that tell more about the main idea.

Some regions of the United States get more rain than others. It rains the most on the northwest coast of the United States. The southeast region gets a lot of rain, too. The region that gets the least rain is the southwest.

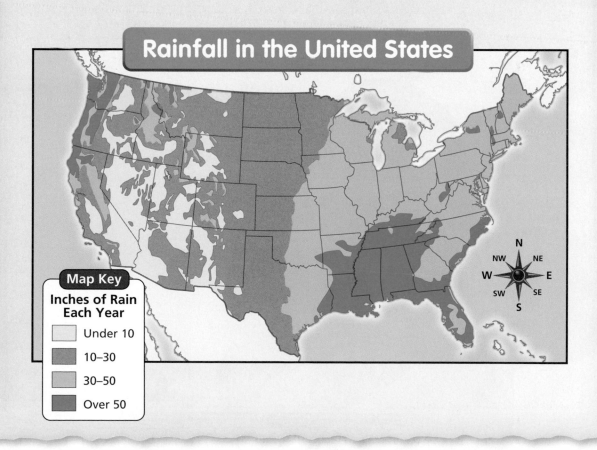

Rainfall in the United States

Map Key
Inches of Rain Each Year
Under 10
10–30
30–50
Over 50

Resources

Build on What You Know

Do you have plants in your classroom? What do plants need to grow? Most plants need air, soil, water, and sunlight. These things are all found in nature. People did not make them.

Different Kinds of Resources

People use different kinds of resources. Like plants, people use things from nature. Something in nature that people use is called a **natural resource.** Air, soil, and water are natural resources. So are trees, rocks, oil, and some kinds of rubber.

Vocabulary

natural resource
environment

Reading Skill

Sequence

STANDARDS

Core: HSS 2.2.4, 2.4, 2.4.3
Extend support: 2.4.3, Analysis Skill HI 2

A woman cuts the bark of rubber trees to get the liquid from which natural rubber is made.

Resources and You

What do people do when a natural resource such as water is scarce? They have to limit the amount of water they use.

Some businesses depend on natural resources to make products. A rubber ball factory needs natural rubber. The business is limited on how many rubber balls it can make by the amount of rubber it can buy. If the supply of rubber is low or runs out, the business might have to make a product that uses a different resource.

(main ★ idea)

Review What natural resource do you use every day?

Can People Get More of It?

Some natural resources can be replaced. Others cannot be replaced. If you cut down a tree, you can plant another one. But if you keep pumping oil out of a well, someday it will run dry. You cannot get more oil from the same place. You might look for oil somewhere else.

main ★ idea

Resources that can be replaced

Trees

Resources that cannot be replaced

Oil

Review What is another resource that can be replaced?

Changing the Environment

main idea

The natural world around you is called the **environment.** Land, water, plants, animals, and people are all part of the environment. People change their environment. To build homes, roads, and businesses in urban, suburban, or rural areas, people cut down trees or smooth away hills. They drill wells for water, build dams across rivers, and drain swamps.

Frame a house.

Cut the trees.

Clear the land.

Consequences

Everything people do to the land and resources (★) main idea has a consequence. A consequence is a result of an action. For example, one important resource in our environment is plants. The roots of trees and other plants help hold the soil down. If you cut down trees, the soil may blow away in the wind. Rain may wash away soil. Losing soil is a consequence of people's actions.

People have planted trees to replace some of the ones they cut down.

People recycle paper, plastic, and metals to save resources.

In the past, people did many things to hurt the environment. Some countries made laws to protect the environment. Countries had to start to clean up the land and water. They had to find ways to keep the air and water clean. Because of the laws and actions in some countries, parts of the world's environments are cleaner today.

Lesson Review

❶ **Vocabulary** Write a sentence explaining how you use a **natural resource.**

❷ **Main Idea** What is one thing people can do when a natural resource becomes scarce?

➤ **Activity** Write a summary of the ideas on pages 104 and 105.

1. HSS 2.4 2. HSS 2.4.3 **Activity** HSS 2.4

Maple Talk

Think of ways that trees are natural resources. Read about **natural resources** in the poem "Maple Talk" from **Poems Have Roots** by Lilian Moore.

Plant us.
Let our roots go
deeply down.
We'll hold the soil
when rain tugs
at the earth.

Plant us.
You will better know
how seasons come
and go.

Watch for
    our leaves unfurling
    in spring green,
    our leafy roofs of summer
    over pools of shade
    our sunset red and gold
    igniting autumn's blaze.

When cold winds
leave us bare
we'll show you treetop nests
where songbirds hid
their young.

And when
in early spring
the sweet sap flows again,
have syrup for your pancakes!

Plant us.

Activities

1. **Talk About It** What are two ways that the maple tree is useful to people?

2. **Make a List** Find as many natural resources in the poem as you can.

Big Ideas

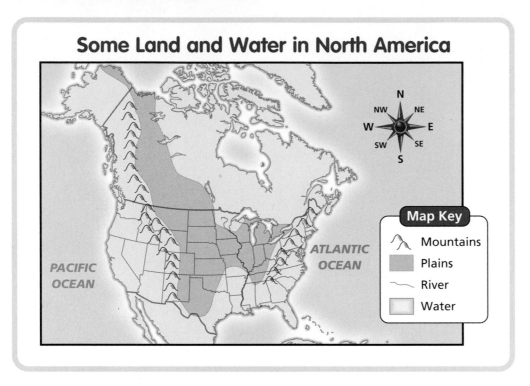

Some Land and Water in North America

PACIFIC OCEAN

ATLANTIC OCEAN

Map Key
- Mountains
- Plains
- River
- Water

What are the missing words?

1. The map shows part of the _____ of North America. 2. A body of water on this map is _____. 3. A landform shown is _____.

 STANDARDS 1. HSS 2.2 2. HSS 2.2 3. HSS 2.2

Facts and Main Ideas

4. Which kind of landform has water all around it? (page 76)

5. How are weather and climate related? (pages 84, 85)

6. Describe two types of regions. (page 92)

7. Name a natural resource that can be replaced. (page 102)

4. HSS 2.2.2 5. Analysis Skill HI 2 6. Analysis Skill HI 2 7. HSS 2.4.3

Vocabulary

Choose the missing word in each sentence.

8. A _____ is low land between hills or mountains.

9. A nation may also be called a _____.

10. The _____ is the natural world around us.

11. A landform that has water on three sides is a _____.

8. HSS 2.2.2 9. HSS 2.2.2 10. HSS 2.2.2 11. HSS 2.2.2 12. HSS 2.4

A. **country** (page 67)

B. **region** (page 92)

C. **valley** (page 75)

D. **peninsula** (page 76)

E. **environment** (page 103)

 Test Practice

12. What do the words **natural resource** mean?

A. something that people make

B. something in nature that people use

C. a place where people cannot live

D. something that can never be replaced

Critical Thinking

Compare and Contrast

13. Describe a way that people have harmed the environment.

14. Describe a way that people have cared for the environment.

13. HSS 2.2.4 14. HSS 2.2.4

Review

Skillbuilders **Parts of a Globe**

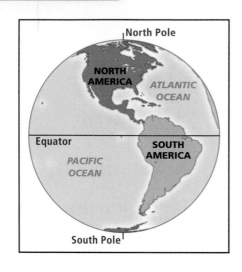

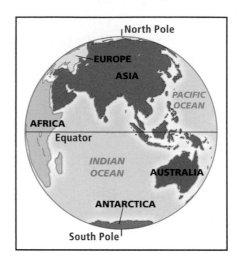

15. What are two bodies of water on the globe?

16. Which two continents are completely in the Southern Hemisphere?

17. On a globe, the equator passes through three continents. Which three are they?

15. HSS 2.2 **16.** HSS 2.2 **17.** HSS 2.2

Use Intermediate Directions

18. In which direction do you go to get from Phoenix, Arizona, to Carson City, Nevada?

19. If you go southeast from Salt Lake City, which city do you reach first?

18. HSS 2.2.2 **19.** HSS 2.2

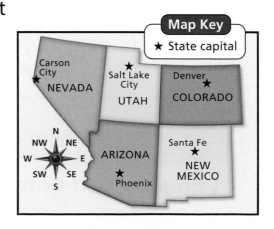

Unit Activity

The Big Idea

Keep a Weather Log

Keep track of the weather for a week. Use that information to make a weather log.

❶ Record the temperature each day.

❷ Note whether it is cloudy, sunny, raining, or snowing.

❸ Make a weather map for one day to go with your log.

Current Events

Current Events Project

Find information about places in your region. Make a **3-D Landform Map.**

The Sierra Nevada Mountains

Technology

Read articles about current events at **www.eduplace.com/kids/hmss/**

In Your Classroom

Look for these Social Studies Independent Books in your classroom.

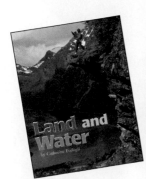

At the Library

You may find these books at your school or public library.

Mountains

By Claire Llewellyn

Hottest, Coldest, Highest, Deepest

By Steve Jenkins

UNIT 3

Ways of Living

"The world's a lovely
Place to be
Because we are
A family."

Mary Ann Hoberman,
from the poem "Our Family"

The Big Idea

What are some of
the cultures that make
up your community,
state, and nation?

Vocabulary Preview

Technology

e • **glossary**
e • **word games**
www.eduplace.com/kids/hmss/

culture

Culture is the way of life of a group of people. Stories are a part of culture. page 117

tradition

A **tradition,** such as Thanksgiving, is something that people do the same way year after year. page 126

Reading Strategy

Use the **summarize** reading strategy in Lessons 1 and 2 and the **predict and infer** strategy in Lessons 3 and 4.

memorial

A **memorial** honors a hero or an event. The Crazy Horse Memorial honors a chief of the Lakota people. page 140

landmark

The Golden Gate Bridge is a San Francisco landmark. A **landmark** is something that helps people know a place. page 138

Families from Many Places

Vocabulary

custom
culture
immigrant
ancestor

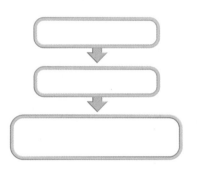

Reading Skill

Draw Conclusions

STANDARDS

Core: HSS 2.1.1, 2.2.3, Analysis Skill REPV 1, 2
Extend support: Analysis Skill REPV 1

Build on What You Know

What are some special times when your family meets with other families or with relatives?

Family Customs

A **custom** is a ceremony or special activity shared among groups of people. Most families have customs. Look at examples on these pages.

main ★ idea

Mary's family sings in church on Sundays.

Families and Cultures

Culture is the way of life of a group of people. The clothes you wear and the foods you eat are part of your culture. Music and language are part of culture. Your religion and your customs are part of your culture too. You learn about your culture from your family, by doing things and by talking together.

Carla's grandma always makes a piñata for her birthday.

Review What is a custom that is part of a culture you know?

Many Cultures in One Country

The United States has many different cultures. Some cultures come from American Indian groups. Some cultures come from immigrant groups. **Immigrants** are people who move from one country to live in another. Many immigrants have come to the United States for freedom. Immigrants from many countries have brought their ways of living to the United States.

A Chinese New Year's Day parade in San Francisco.

Many American Indian groups celebrate their cultures in powwows like this one in Havre, Montana.

Hmong dancers bring their customs to the Tamejavi Festival in Fresno, California.

Review What are two celebrations that came from immigrant groups?

Cultures from Ancestors

An **ancestor** is someone in your family who lived before you were born. <u>You can learn about your culture by learning about your ancestors.</u> You can learn from old pictures of them. You can also look at things that once belonged to them, such as letters or toys. Even your name can tell about your ancestors and their cultures.

main (★) idea

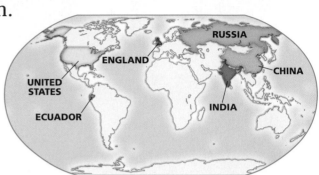

My first name, Kumar, comes from India, where my mother was born. My last name, Bloomstein, comes from Russia, where my father's grandparents were born.

My first name is Isabel, from my mama's Latina family from **Ecuador**. My middle name is Taysin, from my mama's Chinese culture. My last name is Carter, from my father's ancestors in **England**.

Review What is one way that children can learn about their ancestors?

Lesson Review

❶ **Vocabulary** Tell something about the United States using the words **immigrant** and **ancestor**.

❷ **Main Idea** From whom do you learn your culture?

✎ **Activity** Write a paragraph telling when, where, and why your family moved to your local community. Use a map to show where your family came from.

Immigrants at Ellis Island

A boy named Yehuda (yeh HOO duh) came to America from Russia in 1922. Visit Ellis Island with him.

Yehuda saw a man approaching with a big bucket filled with milk and a basket of long yellow fruit. He was stopping at every child, giving each one a cup of milk and one of the strange pieces of fruit. Yehuda watched as one boy bit right into the yellow skin, made a face, and spit it out. Then he saw someone pull the skin down in strips and eat the soft, white fruit inside. Yehuda smiled to himself—every day in America he was learning something new!

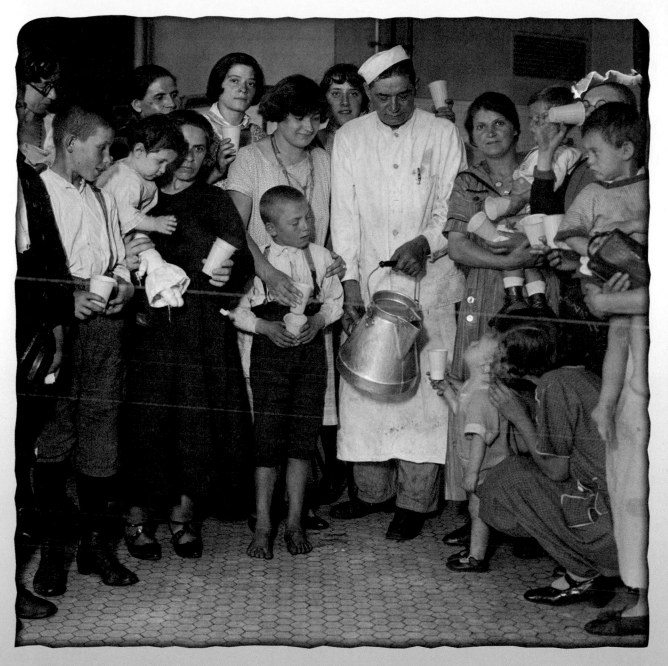

Women and children at Ellis Island getting snacks

Activities

1. **Act It Out** Role-play the story about getting fruit and milk.

2. **Write About It** Describe the face, hair, and clothes of a person in the picture.

Read a Timeline

► **Vocabulary**

timeline

Every family has a history. A timeline can show events in a family's history. A **timeline** is an ordered group of words and dates that shows when events happened.

Look at the timeline of Andrea's family.

Learn the Skill

Step 1 The title tells what the timeline is about. The timeline has a line divided in equal parts. Each part stands for 10 years.

Step 2 Look at the first and last numbers on the timeline. The numbers are years. The events on the timeline happened between these years.

Step 3 The numbers with the events on the timeline tell the year in which each event happened.

1930   1940   1950

1946
Andrea's grandfather is born.

1935
Andrea's great-grandmother comes to the United States from Japan.

Practice the Skill

STANDARDS HSS 2.1.3, Analysis Skill CST 1

Use the timeline to answer the questions below.

1 Was Andrea's grandfather born before, or after, her great-grandmother came to the United States?

2 When did Andrea's great-grandmother come to the United States?

3 Make a timeline of important events in your life.

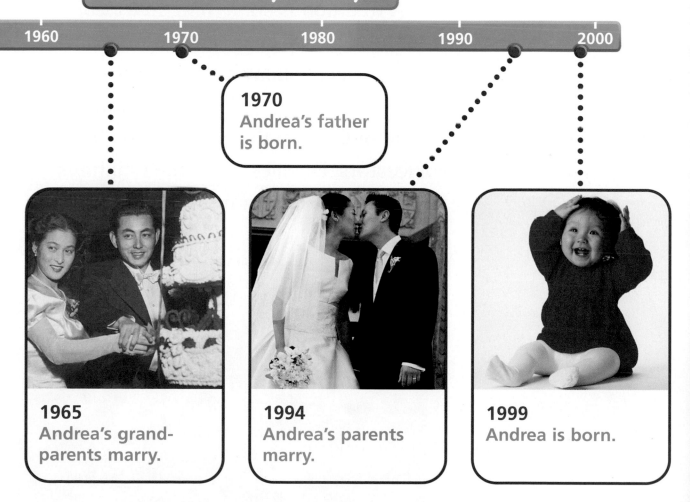

Andrea's Family History

1960   1970   1980   1990   2000

1970
Andrea's father is born.

1965
Andrea's grandparents marry.

1994
Andrea's parents marry.

1999
Andrea is born.

Sharing Cultures

Build on What You Know

Have you sung songs with words in another language? When people share songs of different languages, they share cultures.

Traditions from Cultures

A **tradition** is something that people do the same way year after year. It might be a special holiday meal or clothes for an event. Often families keep a tradition that comes from the culture of their ancestors. Families share their cultures by sharing their traditions with others.

Vocabulary

tradition
legend

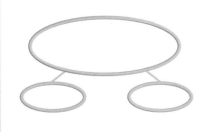

Reading Skill

Main Idea and Details

STANDARDS
Core: HSS 2.1, Analysis Skill CST 3
Extend support: Analysis Skill CST 3

main idea

Sharing Traditions

Izumi's (ih zoo mihz) grandmother learned origami, a paper-folding tradition, from her parents in Japan. She taught it to Izumi. Together they taught origami to other children in Izumi's class.

Review What traditions do you follow in your family?

Sharing Stories and Art

Every culture has stories. People share their cultures by sharing stories called legends. A **legend** is a story that people have passed along for years and years. Many legends come from a time when people told stories but did not write them. Later, people wrote them in books.

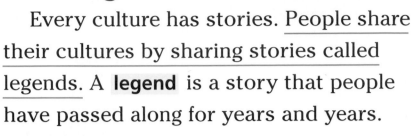

"The Fox and the Crab" is a legend from China. It is in a book of legends from many different countries.

Art is another way of sharing cultures. (★) main idea
People can see art in many different places.

Review What are two ways of sharing culture?

Thomas Hart Benton was famous for painting scenes from the Midwest, such as this painting called "The Boy."

Indians of the Pacific coast carved beautiful totem poles like this.

Artists Who Teach

Some artists share their culture by teaching. Alan Hezekiah (hehz ih KEYE uh) is a musician who teaches drumming to children and adults. Alicia Adame-Molinar (ah LEE see uh ad DAHM ay MOH lee nahr) teaches Mexican dances.

"Drums are in every culture, all around the world. I always wanted to be a drummer. I chose to play drums from Africa because I am an African American. When I play my drum I feel that I am connecting across the oceans, across the years!"

"I was born in Mexico, where music and dancing are very important. I learned many dances when I was growing up. Now I want to share my culture with people in this country. They can learn so much about Mexico when they learn the music and dances!"

Review What is one way that the drummer and dancer on these pages are alike?

Lesson Review

❶ **Vocabulary** Write or tell an example of a **legend** and an example of a **tradition.**

❷ **Main Idea** How can one family learn about another family's culture?

Activity Draw a picture of someone who has shared his or her culture with you. Tell about your picture.

1. Analysis Skill CST 3   **2.** Analysis Skill CST 3   **Activity** Analysis Skill CST 3

Citizenship

Yo-Yo Ma

Yo-Yo Ma was only four years old when he learned to play a cello (CHEHL OH). While still a boy, Yo-Yo Ma moved with his family from France to the United States. He kept studying the cello. His music amazed people.

Yo-Yo Ma plays with musicians from other cultures. He believes that music helps people from all cultures understand one another.

Sharing Musical Traditions

As a grownup, Yo-Yo Ma has become a famous musician. He has played concerts around the world. He is excited about music from many cultures. In 1998, he started bringing together musicians from many cultures. They share their musical **traditions.** They learn from one another and make new music too.

Today Yo-Yo Ma is a U.S. citizen.

Activities

1. **Discuss It** Why does Yo-Yo Ma want musicians to share traditions?

2. **Write About It** Write or tell two things you learned about Yo-Yo Ma.

Technology More biographies at www.eduplace.com/kids/hmss/

Skillbuilder

Conduct an Interview

▶ **Vocabulary**
interview

In an **interview,** a reporter asks a person questions about a topic.

Learn the Skill

Interview a grandparent or another older person in your family. What would you like to know about that person's past or traditions?

Step 1 Prepare your interview questions. Write four or five questions you can ask. Good questions start with words like **who, what, where, when, how, why,** and **what kind of.** For example, **How was life the same as or different from today?**

Step 2 Practice asking your interview questions. Ask one question at a time.

Step 3 You may want to rewrite some of your questions.

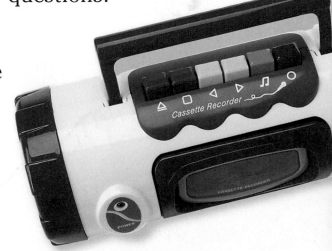

Cassette Recorder

Practice the Skill

Set up a time to do your interview. Then follow the directions.

❶ Think about what you want to know. Write your questions. Decide the order in which you wish to ask them.

❷ Bring a notebook and pencil so that you can take notes. If possible, bring a tape recorder.

❸ Be polite. Listen carefully to each answer. Thank the person when you are finished.

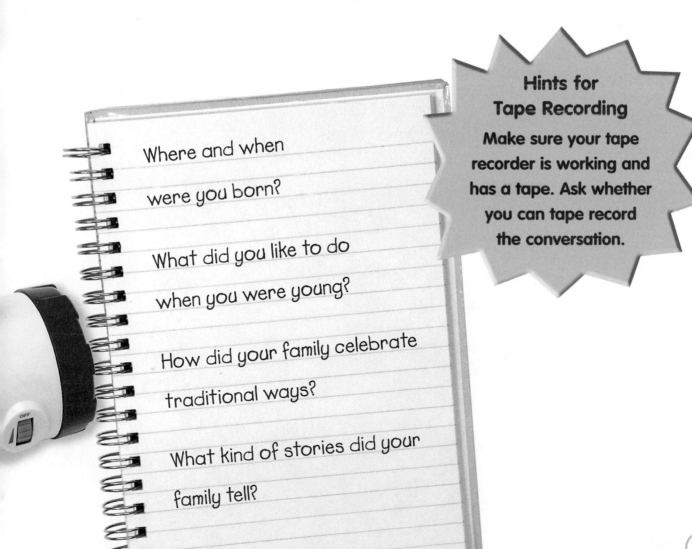

Hints for Tape Recording

Make sure your tape recorder is working and has a tape. Ask whether you can tape record the conversation.

Where and when were you born?

What did you like to do when you were young?

How did your family celebrate traditional ways?

What kind of stories did your family tell?

America's Symbols

Vocabulary

landmark
President
monument
memorial

Reading Skill

Classify

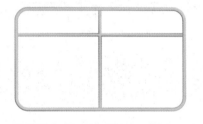

STANDARDS

Core: HSS 2.5
Extend support: HSS 2.5

Build on What You Know What would you put in a picture to stand for the United States? Pictures, buildings, and statues can stand for a country.

Culture and Symbols

In the United States, people have traditions that have come from many cultures. They also share traditions that began in this country. The United States has a culture from those traditions.

What are some symbols in the seal of the President of the United States?

A symbol is a picture, place, or thing that stands for something else. For example, a picture of a bicycle may be a symbol for a bike path.

Symbols for the United States remind people that they are part of one country. The American flag is the symbol people use most often for the United States.

main idea

Review Why are symbols for the United States important to people who live here?

Uncle Sam

137

American Landmarks

A **landmark** is something that helps people know a place. A sign or statue may be a landmark. Many landmarks are symbols for America. Look at some on these pages. The map shows where they are.

Landmarks in the United States

Mount Rushmore
Black Hills, South Dakota

The leader of the United States of America is called the **President.** An artist and many helpers carved the faces of four important Presidents in the stone of this mountain. The faces are 60 feet high!

George Washington

Thomas Jefferson

Theodore Roosevelt

Abraham Lincoln

Statue of Liberty
New York Bay, New York

This statue is the size of a tall building. A French artist sent the great statue as a gift of friendship from his country more than a hundred years ago. The statue still welcomes immigrants and visitors to America.

Liberty Bell
Philadelphia, Pennsylvania

Americans rang this bell at the start of their new country in 1776. You can still visit it in Philadelphia. Pictures of the Liberty Bell are symbols for freedom in America.

Review Why is the Statue of Liberty an important landmark?

Monuments and Memorials

Many buildings and statues honor heroes or events. Some are called **monuments.** Others are called **memorials.** Both can be landmarks. Monuments and memorials help people remember. These monuments and memorials are in Washington, D.C.

Lincoln Memorial

Abraham Lincoln was the President of the United States during the Civil War. Two of his best known speeches are printed on the walls of the memorial.

Washington Monument

The Washington Monument honors George Washington. He was the first President of the United States. He was known for being brave, strong, and honest.

Thomas Jefferson Memorial

Thomas Jefferson was the third President. He wrote the Declaration of Independence. That was the paper that said that the United States should have freedom from Great Britain. Some of his words are printed on the walls of the memorial.

Review Why do people build monuments and memorials to Presidents?

Lesson Review

❶ Vocabulary Tell what is the same about **monuments** and **memorials.**

❷ Main Idea What are some symbols that remind us that we are all members of one country?

HANDS ON **Activity** Draw one of the symbols of the United States. Tell what you think and feel about the symbol.

The Star-Spangled Banner

The year was 1814. The United States was at war. All night Francis Scott Key watched the British fire cannons at an American fort. Its flag stayed up during the battle. This proved to Key that the United States was strong. He was so proud, he wrote a poem.

The poem that Key wrote was set to music. It became the anthem of the United States. An anthem is a song that is a **symbol** of a place.

Fort McHenry in Baltimore, Maryland

The Star-Spangled Banner

Oh, say can you see, by the dawn's early
light,

What so proudly we hailed at the twilight's
last gleaming?

Whose broad stripes and bright stars,
through the perilous fight,

O'er the ramparts we watched, were so
gallantly streaming?

And the rockets' red glare, the bombs
bursting in air,

Gave proof through the night that
our flag was still there.

O say, does that star-spangled
banner yet wave

O'er the land of the free and the
home of the brave?

Activities

1. **Talk About It** Explain how a song can be a
symbol of a country.

2. **Write About It** Choose a line of words in the
song and tell what you think the words mean.

We Celebrate Holidays

Vocabulary
national holiday
religious holiday

Reading Skill
Classify

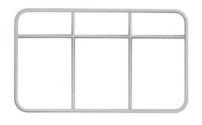

STANDARDS
Core: HSS 2.5, Analysis Skill CST 3
Extend support: HSS 2.5

Build on What You Know Name some holidays you celebrate. Find out how holidays are alike and different.

National Holidays

A holiday is a day that honors a person or an event. A **national holiday** honors someone or something that is important to the country. The date for a national holiday is the same everywhere in the country. Schools and many workplaces are closed so that families and friends can celebrate together.

main idea (★)

Presidents' Day is a national holiday that honors two American Presidents, George Washington and Abraham Lincoln.

State Holidays

Some holidays are state holidays. A state holiday usually honors an event or a person who is important to that state. Schools and workplaces may be closed, but only in the state where people celebrate that holiday. In California, for example, people celebrate Cesar Chavez Day of Service and Learning.

Review What is a way that state holidays are different from national holidays?

Massachusetts and Maine celebrate Patriots' Day. It honors events that took place in those states during the American Revolution.

Religious Holidays

People who belong to a religion share a set of beliefs. They may have times to honor events that go with the beliefs of their religion. These times are called **religious holidays.** Some traditions of religious holidays are passed down from our ancestors.

Ramadan

For the month of Ramadan, Muslims do not eat or drink during the day. They say prayers at certain times. After sunset, they eat together.

Easter

For Easter, Christians say special prayers in church. Some Christians give up certain foods for a time before Easter.

Passover

For Passover, Jews have a meal called a seder, with prayers, songs, and symbols. For about a week, Jews do not eat most kinds of bread, cakes, or cookies.

Review What things do people do on religious holidays?

Other Holidays

Some holidays are not religious, state, or national holidays. Some holidays honor traditions of a culture.

A Saint Patrick's Day parade

Lesson Review

❶ **Vocabulary** Write a sentence about a **religious holiday** and a sentence about a **national holiday.**

❷ **Main Idea** Explain how a national holiday is different from a religious holiday.

Activity Draw a picture of people celebrating a holiday you like. Tell if it is a national, state, or religious holiday.

1. Analysis Skill CST 3 **2.** Analysis Skill CST 3 **Activity** Analysis Skill CST 3

Cesar Chavez

When Cesar Chavez was ten, his life changed for the worse. His family lost their home and became farm workers. Both grownups and children worked very hard in fields for very low pay. Often they were treated unfairly.

Cesar Chavez wanted to change how farm workers were treated. As a grownup in California, he led farm workers in their struggle for better pay and safety. Chavez was a strong, caring leader. He often said, "¡Si se puede!" (see say PWAY day). It means "Yes we can!" People believed in him. In California many schools do service projects on the state holiday that honors him.

Activities

1. **Discuss It** What did Chavez do to help make things more fair?

2. **Write About It** Write or tell about a service project children could do or have done in your school.

Technology Read more biographies at www.eduplace.com/kids/hmss/

Citizenship Skills

Skillbuilder

Make a Decision

▶ **Vocabulary**

decision

To make a **decision,** you make up your mind. It may help to compare choices in a chart.

Learn the Skill

Suppose that your class wants to do a project that helps the school. Many children like two different ideas. How do you make a decision about which idea is best for the school?

Step 1 Put the ideas in a chart that shows what is good and not good about each choice. Use plus (+) for good and minus (-) for not good.

Step 2 Think and talk about what is good and not good about each choice. Write your thoughts in the chart.

Step 3 Compare choices in the chart. You might ask: Which choice will help more people in the school? Decide which choice is better.

School Clean-up Day	School Garden
✚	✚
School will look better. More school pride	Beautiful flowers Healthful vegetables
▬	▬
Hard work Not fun	Takes too long. Might not grow.

STANDARDS Analysis Skill HI 4

Practice the Skill

Follow the directions to help Nino make a decision.

1 Look at the pictures and read the words. Tell what Nino's choices are.

2 Make a chart to show what is good about each choice and what is not good about each choice.

3 Think of a question Nino might ask to help him decide. Use the question and the chart to make a choice.

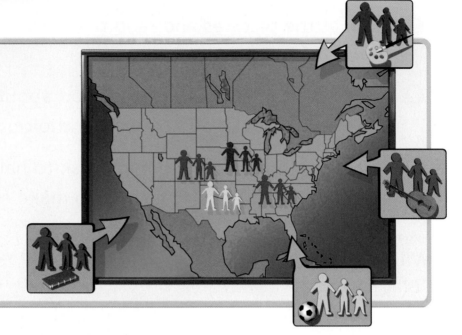

American Culture

- **Your Family**

- **Your Country**

- **The World**

Choose words that help describe the picture.

Your culture comes from your **1.** _____ and your **2.** _____.
Languages and traditions are part of **3.** _____ .

STANDARDS **1.** Analysis Skill CST 3   **2.** Analysis Skill CST 3   **3.** Analysis Skill CST 3

Facts and Main Ideas

4. In what way do immigrants change American culture?
   (pages 118, 119)

5. What are two languages that people might speak in the
   United States? (pages 118–121)

6. Who has been honored by an American monument or
   memorial? (pages 138, 140–141)

7. What are two symbols of the United States? (page 139)

8. What is one tradition that is part of a religious holiday? (page 146)

4. Analysis Skill HI 2   **5.** HSS 2.1.1   **6.** HSS 2.5   **7.** HSS 2.5   **8.** Analysis Skill CST 3

Vocabulary

Choose the letter of the word to match the correct sentence.

9. A story that has been passed along for a long time

10. Something that people keep doing in the same way

11. A person who lived before us

12. A building or monument that helps people know a place

9. Analysis Skill CST 3 10. Analysis Skill CST 3 11. HSS 2.1
12. Analysis Skill HI 2 13. Analysis Skill CST 3

A. **ancestor** (page 120)

B. **landmark** (page 138)

C. **legend** (page 128)

D. **immigrant** (page 118)

E. **tradition** (page 126)

 Test Practice

13. What do the words **national holiday** mean?

   A. a special day for people of a religion

   B. a day when events or people important to a state are honored

   C. a day when events or people important to a nation are honored

   D. a building that honors a famous person

Critical Thinking

Classify

14. Name a state holiday and tell why people celebrate it.

14. Analysis Skill CST 3

153

Review

Skillbuilders   **Read a Timeline**

Dan's Life History

Dan was born   Dan learned to read   Dan today

15. How old is Dan today?

16. What did Dan do when he was six?

15. Analysis Skill CST 1 **16.** Analysis Skill CST 1

Make a Decision

17. What can Nora do? Name two or three choices.

18. Make a chart for each choice to show what is good or bad about it.

Good	Bad

19. What should Nora choose? Tell reasons for your decision.

17. Analysis Skill HI 4 **18.** Analysis Skill HI 4 **19.** Analysis Skill HI 4

Unit Activity

 The Big Idea

Culture Banner

Use pictures to make an American culture banner that shows the many people and symbols that make up our country's culture.

❶ Draw or bring in pictures to put on the banner.

❷ Write a title and your name on the banner.

❸ Arrange the pictures on your banner.

Current Events

Current Events Project

What celebrations are taking place in your community? Make an exhibit about **Celebrations in the News.**

 Technology

Read articles about current events at **www.eduplace.com/kids/hmss/**

In Your Classroom

Look for these Social Studies Independent Books in your classroom.

At the Library

You may find these books at your school or public library.

Grandma Maxine Remembers
by Ann Morris

Everybody Brings Noodles
by Norah Dooley

UNIT 4

People at Work

"At Dudley Market
now I tell
Most kinds of articles
they sell:
Hats, caps and bonnets blue
And trousers wide
enough for two"

Ben Boucher, from the poem
"Dudley Market," 1827

The Big Idea

What are ways
people earn, spend,
and save money?

Vocabulary Preview

Technology
e • **glossary**
e • **word games**
www.eduplace.com/kids/hmss/

producer

A **producer** is someone who provides a service or makes goods. Julie has a dogwalking service, so she is a producer. page 166

consumer

A **consumer** is someone who buys goods or services. You are a consumer when you buy crayons. page 166

Reading Strategy

Use the **question** reading strategy in Lessons 1, 2, and 3 and the **summarize** strategy in Lessons 4, 5, and 6.

income

The money people earn when they work is their **income.** Sam's income is the $5.00 he earns each week on his paper route.

page 168

price

Price is the amount of money you pay to buy something. If you look in two or three stores, you may find the same toy at different prices. page 180

Needs, Wants, and Choices

Vocabulary

needs

shelter

wants

 **Reading Skill**

Predict Outcomes

STANDARDS

Core: HSS 2.4
Extend support: HSS 2.4

Build on What You Know

Have you bought anything at a store? What choices did you make?

Needs and Wants

Needs are things that people must have to live. Everyone has to have food, water, clothing, and **shelter.** Shelter is something that protects or covers. Houses, trailer homes, and apartments are kinds of shelter.

Wants are things that people would like to have. People do not have to have those things to live. Everyone has wants and needs.

main idea

Making Choices

People cannot have everything they want. <u>People</u> <u>have to make choices about what to buy.</u> If they use all their money to buy one thing, they cannot buy something else.

> I have $30 saved. I can buy a computer game and play with it today. Or I can buy a scooter and ride it in the spring.

Sally's Choices

Choices	What I Give Up	What I Get
Buy computer game	Ride scooter in spring	Enjoy computer game today
Buy scooter	Enjoy computer game today	Ride scooter in spring

Review If Sally buys the computer game, what does she give up?

Lesson Review

❶ **Vocabulary** Name some **needs** and some **wants**.

❷ **Main Idea** Which would you choose, the game or the scooter? Why?

✏ **Activity** Write a summary for this lesson.

1. HSS 2.4 2. HSS 2.4 **Activity** HSS 2.4

THE MILKMAID

"The Milkmaid" is a tale told in Mexico and many other countries.

❖ ❖ ❖

Maria was a milkmaid who worked for a rich family. Sometimes the family gave Maria their leftover milk. Maria made extra money by selling the milk. One day the family gave Maria enough milk to fill a big jug.

On her way to market to sell the milk she thought, "I will have money to buy a hen that will lay many eggs. I will sell the eggs and use the money to buy a pig."

"When the pig has grown large, I will sell it and buy a cow. My cow will always give me milk to sell."

Maria thought of all the money she would make, and skipped with joy. Then, oops! Down she fell! Crash went the milk jug! Out spilled the milk, and with it Maria's dreams.

Maria cried and cried. Finally she said, "I may not get all I wanted, but I still have what I need."

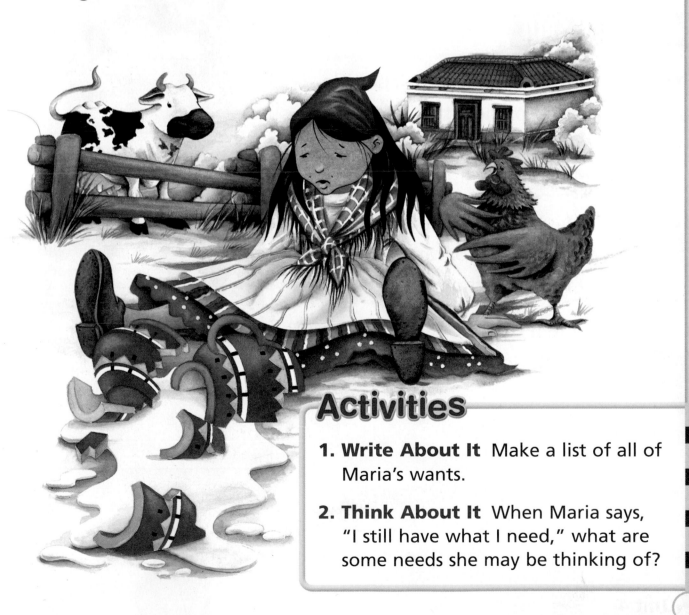

Activities

1. **Write About It** Make a list of all of Maria's wants.

2. **Think About It** When Maria says, "I still have what I need," what are some needs she may be thinking of?

Reading and Thinking Skills

Compare Fact and Fiction

Fiction books are about made-up things. **Nonfiction** books tell facts. A **fact** is something that is true.

► **Vocabulary**

fiction

nonfiction

fact

Learn the Skill

Step 1 Read the book cover. The title and photo show that the book is a true story about a real family farm.

Step 2 The words in this book tell facts. The photographs show real things and people.

Step 3 Decide if the book is fiction, or nonfiction. Tell why you think so.

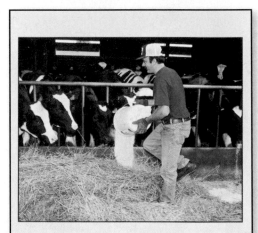

Mr. Koebel is in charge of the cows, or the herd. He is called the herdsman.

10

STANDARDS Analysis Skill REPV 3

Practice the Skill

Follow the directions.

1 Look at the book titles below. Which book is fiction?

2 Look at the book pages. How can you tell that the fiction book is fiction?

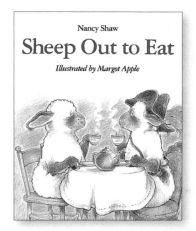

Sheep graze on grass
and other plants.

Sheep chomp. Sheep sneeze.

Work

Vocabulary

producer
consumer
income

Reading Skill
Draw Conclusions

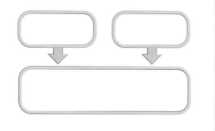

STANDARDS

Core: HSS 2.4.1, 2.4.2
Extend support: HSS 2.4.1

Build on What You Know

Where do you get the things you need and want? Who makes those things?

Getting Things We Need

Hungry? Want an apple to eat? If you are the farmer who grows the apple, you are a **producer.** A producer is a person who makes or grows something. If you are the person who buys the apple and eats it, you are a **consumer.** A consumer is someone who buys or uses things.

What if you grow the apple and eat the apple?
Then you are a producer and a consumer.

Review In what ways are you a consumer?

I am a producer. I make lemonade and sell it.

I am a consumer. I buy the lemonade and drink it. Yummy!

Ways to Earn Money

When people work, they usually earn money. This money is their **income.**

One person's income may be earned from selling a painting he made. Another person may earn money by selling a crop she grew. Sometimes people sell their skills or their time. They are paid for teaching in a school or working in a shop. <u>People do different kinds of work.</u>

main idea

I own a small business. I like to help people with computer problems. I also like being my own boss!

I run this machine. I am really good at making cars.

I work all day. At night, I go to school. I want to be a chef and make really tasty meals for people!

I like to make people's homes look beautiful.

Review What work do people do to earn money?

Lesson Review

❶ **Vocabulary** Name two ways to earn **income.**

❷ **Main Idea** What is a way that someone can be both a producer and a consumer?

Activity Draw a picture that shows a job you might like to do someday.

First Farmers

Were people always producers of their food? Look back more than ten thousand years. People did not have cities, towns, or farms. Instead, they moved from place to place. They gathered wild plants to eat.

Then some people took seeds from the strongest wild grains. They planted the seeds. The plants grew well. People picked the grain. They used some of it and saved the rest for planting.

Some of the first farmers lived in Mesopotamia.

2. Planting seeds

Having plants to care for, farmers began to live near their fields. Small towns grew up nearby.

1. Making tools

First farmers needed tools to plant seeds and cut grain.

4. Grinding grain
Farmers ground grain into flour.

5. Baking bread
Flour was made into bread.

3. Harvesting grain
Farmers cut the grain. Some was stored away.

Activities

1. **Chart It** Make a flow chart showing the steps described in the words and pictures on these pages.

2. **Think About It** For thousands of years, people gathered wild grain. Why do you think people decided to grow it instead?

Goods and Services

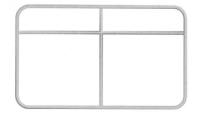
Build on What You Know Have you ever wondered how your clothing was made or who made your toys?

Goods

The things people make or grow are called goods. **Goods** are things that you can touch, such as cars, apples, and baseballs. Many goods are made in a **factory.** A factory is a building where people work to make goods.

These people are working in a shoe factory.

Services

Some people are doctors, teachers, or dogwalkers. Those people do not make things. They provide **services.** Services are activities that people do to help other people.

Review What are some services that you use?

Lesson Review

1 Vocabulary What are some **goods** that you use?

2 Main Idea What is one way goods are different from services?

Activity Make a picture chart showing goods and services.

1. HSS 2.4.2 **2.** HSS 2.4.2 **Activity** HSS 2.4.2

SCIENTISTS SERVING OTHERS

Some scientists discover things that help many people.

Marie Curie had a good memory that helped her as a student in Poland. When she grew up, she became a scientist. She lived and worked in France with her husband Pierre. Together, they made some big discoveries. Other scientists built on their work to find ways of curing sick people and making energy.

Louis Pasteur (LOO ee pas TUR) When Louis Pasteur was a boy, his teacher saw that Louis was patient and hardworking. Later, those qualities helped Pasteur become one of France's most famous scientists. He found that heating milk killed germs. That made the milk safer to drink. Pasteur's discoveries have helped millions of people stay healthy. Milk is still heated today. The process is called pasteurization. (pas chuhr ih ZAY shuhn)

George Washington Carver The plant scientist George Washington Carver wanted to help African American farmers make more money from the crops they grew. After many experiments and much hard work, Carver found hundreds of ways to use peanuts, soybeans, and sweet potatoes. Then, he thought, farmers could earn income by growing these plants too.

Eloy Rodriguez (ee LOY rohd REE gehs) Think on your feet. Use common sense. Eloy Rodriguez often heard that advice in Spanish from his family. Now he is a scientist who studies how animals use plants to heal themselves. From this he has learned ways that plants can heal people. Also, Eloy Rodriguez gets students excited about science. He shares advice that helped him.

Activities

1. **Think About It** What are some ways these scientists show caring for others?

2. **Write About It** Write or tell how people's lives are better because of the work of the scientists you have read about.

Read a Bar Graph

Many foods are produced in the United States. This bar graph shows how much milk cows produce each year.

▶ **Vocabulary**

bar graph

Learn the Skill

Using a **bar graph** is a way to compare things. The bars show how much there is of something.

Step 1 The numbers and words at the side of the graph tell how much. On this graph, the number 30 stands for 30 billion pounds of milk.

Step 2 Along the bottom of the graph are the names of some states in which milk is produced.

Step 3 Look at the bar above California. It goes up to 30. That means that in California, cows produce 30 billion pounds of milk each year. How much milk do cows in Wisconsin produce?

Practice the Skill

Look at the graph below. Then answer the questions.

1 How much milk is produced in New York each year?

2 In which state on the graph is the smallest amount of milk produced?

3 In which state do cows produce more milk each year, Wisconsin or New York?

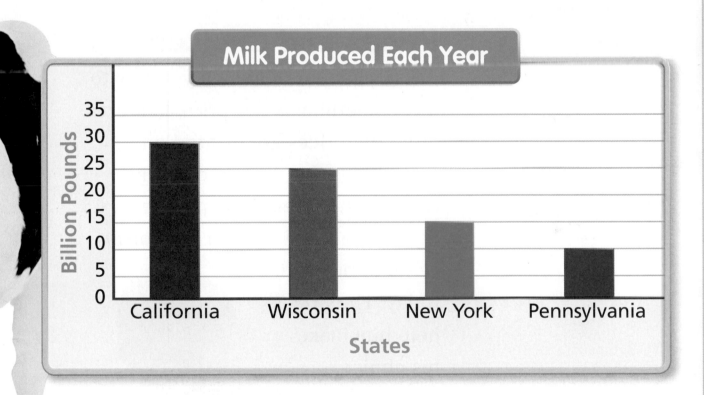

Milk Produced Each Year

States

People Save Money

Build on What You Know

Suppose you are given $2.00 for helping a neighbor. What will you do with it? Will you buy something now, or keep it for later?

Prices and Choices

The amount of money you pay to buy something is the **price.** In stores, often the prices are printed on or near things that people can buy. Looking at prices helps people decide what to buy. Ken has thirty cents to buy fruit today. The prices help him make his choice.

What do you think Ken's choice will be? Why?

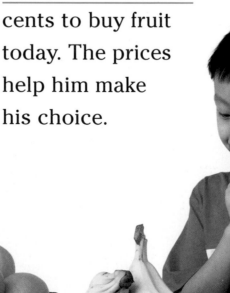

· 30¢ each · 40¢ each · 25¢ each

I'm saving for my children to go to college.

We're saving for a trip to Brazil.

I'm saving up to buy roller skates.

These people tell why they are saving money.

Saving Money

Many people are careful not to spend all their income. Some save money so they can pay for what they want. They might save money in a piggy bank. A **bank** is a safe place where people keep their money.

main idea (★)

Review Why do people save money?

A Savings Account

Most people use a bank that has many services. One service is called a **savings account.** Instead of keeping their money at home, people put it in a savings account. They let the bank use the money. In return, the bank adds a bit more money each month. That money is called interest. Interest helps the amount of money in the account grow.

Review How are banks that are businesses and banks in people's homes alike and different?

What services are in a bank?

Gina Saves

Gina has a savings account at a bank in her town. Last year she put in money every month to save for baseball camp in July. Look at the graph of Gina's account.

Money in Gina's Savings Account

Skill Reading Graphs What do you think Gina did with her money in July?

Lesson Review

❶ **Vocabulary** Describe a **savings account** in a bank.

❷ **Main Idea** What is one reason for saving money in banks that are businesses?

➤ **Activity** Write or tell about a buying choice you have made.

1. HSS 2.4 2. HSS 2.4 **Activity** HSS 2.4

Spend Your Dollar

Welcome to Write On store. Take a look at what is for sale. Compare **prices.** Then see what your dollar will buy.

1 Look at the items. Choose the items you like.

2 You have only $1.00 to spend. Check the prices. See what you can buy with your $1.00.

3 Record on a class chart the items you choose. Add the prices and record the total.

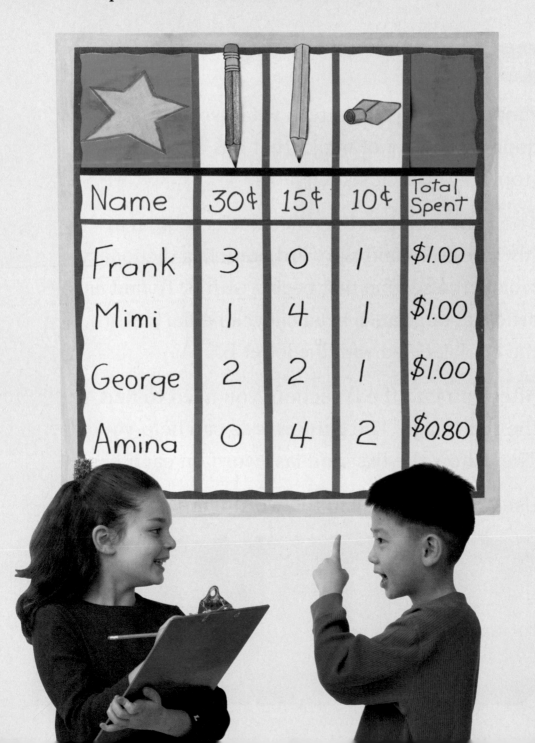

Name	30¢	15¢	10¢	Total Spent
Frank	3	0	1	$1.00
Mimi	1	4	1	$1.00
George	2	2	1	$1.00
Amina	0	4	2	$0.80

Use Reference Books

You can find out more about a topic by using reference books.

▶ **Vocabulary**

dictionary
encyclopedia

Learn the Skill

A **dictionary** is a book that tells what words mean. An **encyclopedia** is a set of books that has articles on different topics. The articles tell facts.

Step 1 The information in reference books is often in ABC order. To find the word **bank** in a dictionary, look in the section that begins with B. To find an article about **banks** in an encyclopedia, look in the book labeled with the letter B.

Step 2 After you find the B section, you need to find the right page. The **guidewords** can help you. They show the first and last word on each page.

Step 3 Use ABC order to find the word **bank.**

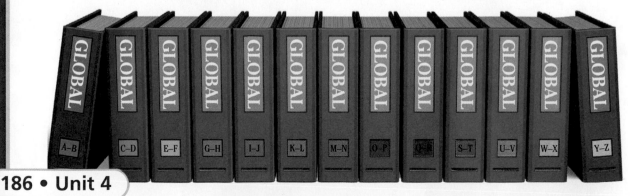

Practice the Skill

Follow the directions.

1 Suppose your teacher asks you to find information about the first factories. Tell which kind of reference book you will use.

2 Use a dictionary to find the definition of these words: **product, income, business**

Guidewords

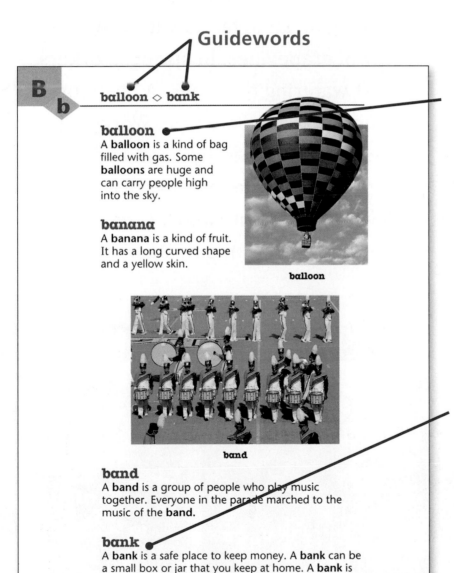

B
b

balloon ◇ bank

balloon
A **balloon** is a kind of bag filled with gas. Some **balloons** are huge and can carry people high into the sky.

banana
A **banana** is a kind of fruit. It has a long curved shape and a yellow skin.

balloon

band

band
A **band** is a group of people who play music together. Everyone in the parade marched to the music of the **band**.

bank
A **bank** is a safe place to keep money. A **bank** can be a small box or jar that you keep at home. A **bank** is also a big building. People can leave money or borrow it at the **bank**.

20

The first word on this page is **balloon.** It is the first guideword.

The last word is **bank.** It is the second guideword.

From Field to Market

Vocabulary

human resource

capital resource

scarcity

Reading Skill

Sequence

STANDARDS

Core: HSS 2.4.1, 2.4.2, 2.4.3
Extend support: HSS 2.4.1, Analysis Skill CST 1, 3

Build on What You Know Do you know how a bunch of grapes becomes the box of raisins in your lunch?

From the Vine to You!

Imagine large farms with row after row of grapevines. In spring, workers start watering the vines. A few months later, the grapes are ripe. Workers pick the grape bunches by hand and place them on clean paper trays. The grapes dry in the sun for two to three weeks. Slowly they become raisins.

Picking grapes

Drying grapes

Workers drive the raisins to the food processing plant. There the raisins are checked and cleaned. Machines take off the stems and package the raisins. Ships, trains, and trucks carry the packages across the country and around the world. Stores sell the raisins to you! It takes many steps to get a box of raisins from a bunch of grapes.

main idea

Review When do grapes become raisins?

Cleaning raisins

Sorting raisins

Boxing raisins

Three Kinds of Resources

Raisin producers in California depend on California's warm weather and natural resources. Producers need sunny days, good soil, and water. Raisin producers also need **human resources.** Human resources are people. They are the farm workers who care for the vines. They are the people who operate machines, sell raisins, and run the business.

Raisin producers need a third kind of resource. They need capital resources. **Capital resources** are things such as tools, machinery, buildings, and trucks. The buildings where raisins are sorted and cleaned are capital resources. So are the machines that take the stems off the raisins. Producers of raisins and other goods use all three kinds of resources.

Resources

Human Resources	Natural Resources	Capital Resources
farm workers sales people machine operators	soil water	machines trucks tools

Scarcity

The three kinds of resources are all limited. The earth has only so many human, natural, and capital resources. However, people have unlimited wants for goods and services. That is why there is scarcity. **Scarcity** means we don't have enough resources to produce all the goods and services we want.

Some farmers choose to use their land to grow grapes.

Some farmers choose to use their land for growing vegetables.

Because we can't have all we want, we have to make choices about what to make or grow. In some parts of California, water is scarce. Farmers make choices about the crops they grow based on the amount of water the crop needs.

Review Why do people have to make choices about what to make or grow?

Lesson Review

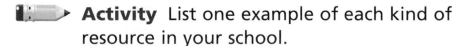

❶ **Vocabulary** Explain what **scarcity** is.

❷ **Main Idea** What are the three kinds of resources people use to produce goods and services?

 Activity List one example of each kind of resource in your school.

1. HSS 2.4.3 **2.** HSS 2.4.2 **Activity** HSS 2.4

193

Keeping Food Cold

A Cool Timeline

For hundreds of years, people have found ways to keep food from spoiling by keeping it cold. There were many ways to keep food cold before people used refrigerators. Look at how the ways have changed.

1750   1800

250 years ago
Settlers dug root cellars inside or outside their homes.

1850	1900	1950	2000

170 years ago

A big block of ice kept food inside the ice box cold. The iceman delivered a new block of ice every other day or so.

80 to 90 years ago

People began using electric refrigerators with freezers.

Activities

1. **Talk About It** Tell a story about a time when the electricity was out and your family could not keep food cold in the refrigerator.

2. **Think About It** What are the costs and benefits of a refrigerator and an ice box?

People and Nations Trade

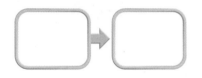

Vocabulary
barter
trade
specialize

Reading Skill
Cause and Effect

STANDARDS
Core: HSS 2.3.2, 2.4
Extend support: HSS 2.4

Build on What You Know

Swapping toys or baseball cards with a friend is one way to get the things you want. What are other ways?

Barter

What you do when you swap toys or cards is called barter. **Barter** takes place when people exchange goods or services without using money. Long ago barter was the main way people got the things they wanted.

main idea

I'll give you this pig for two pounds of beets.

I'll trade one pound of beets for your pig.

Skill **Visual Learning** What do people use to help them trade goods?

Trade

Many times, barter does not work very well. That is why most people today pay for goods and services in other ways, often with money. Whether people barter or use money, they are taking part in trade. <u>**Trade** is the buying and selling of goods and services.</u> You take part in trade when you buy an apple.

Review What is one way you take part in trade?

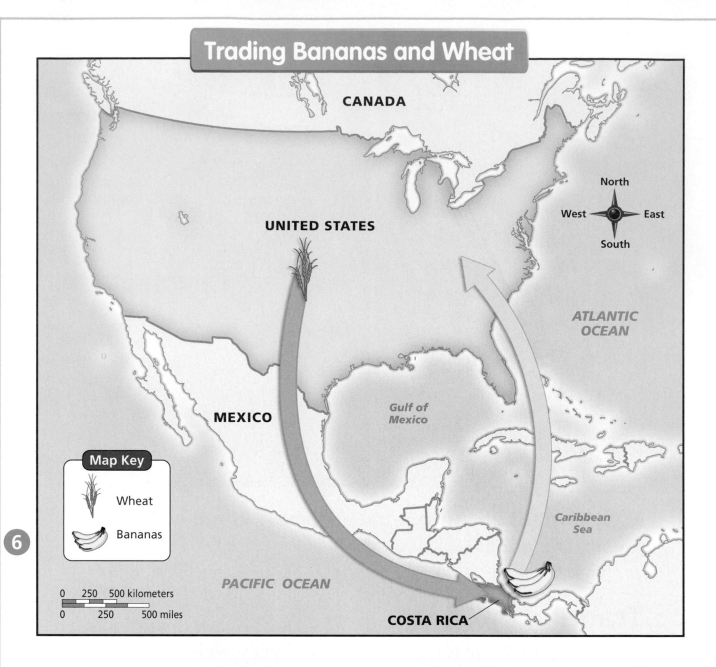

Trading Bananas and Wheat

CANADA

UNITED STATES

North
West • East
South

ATLANTIC
OCEAN

MEXICO

Gulf of
Mexico

Caribbean
Sea

Map Key

Wheat

Bananas

PACIFIC OCEAN

COSTA RICA

0   250   500 kilometers
0   250   500 miles

6

bananas

wheat

Depending on One Another

Farmers in the United States specialize in growing wheat, not bananas. Farmers in Costa Rica specialize in growing bananas, not wheat. When farmers **specialize,** that means they choose to grow mainly one crop. Farmers in the United States sell their wheat to consumers in Costa Rica. Farmers in Costa Rica sell their bananas to consumers in the United States. People in countries around the world depend on trade to get the goods and services they want.

main idea ★

Review What does it mean to specialize?

Lesson Review

❶ **Vocabulary** The buying and selling of goods and services is called _____.

❷ **Main Idea** What is one reason that countries trade with one another?

Activity Write about a time when you exchanged one item for another. Tell the events in order. Use details to make your story clear.

1. HSS 2.4 2. HSS 2.3.2 **Activity** HSS 2.4

199

Geography

Money Around the World

There is an old saying that money cannot buy happiness. That's true, but money does buy a lot of other things. People everywhere use metal coins and paper bills to buy **goods** and **services**.

Countries around the world have their own money. The United States has the dollar. Jordan has the dinar. Find other money names.

The European Union

euro

2-euro coin

Brazil

real

50-centavo coin

Kenya

shilling

5-shilling coin

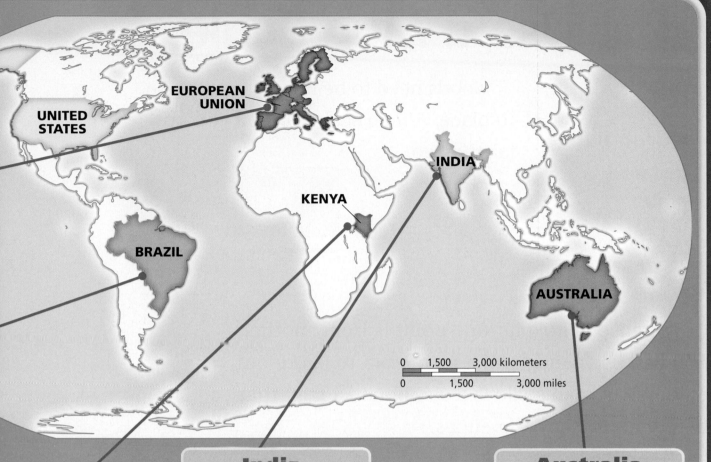

UNITED
STATES

EUROPEAN
UNION

INDIA

KENYA

BRAZIL

AUSTRALIA

0   1,500   3,000 kilometers

0   1,500   3,000 miles

India

rupee

1-paisa coin

Australia

dollar

5-cent coin

Activities

1. **Name It** Which country besides the United States uses a dollar?

2. **Research It** Look up "Money" in an encyclopedia. Find out who is shown on the U.S. penny, nickel, dime, and quarter.

Use a Map Scale

Goods need to be moved from place to place. A map scale can tell you how far they go.

▶ **Vocabulary**

distance

scale

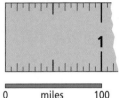

0   miles   100

Learn the Skill

Distance is how far one point is from another. You can use a map and a map **scale** to figure out distance. A map scale is a symbol on a map that can help you measure distances.

Step 1 Look at the map scale and the ruler. The blue scale bar measures one inch.

Step 2 Look at the numbers on the scale. They show that one inch on the map stands for 100 miles. How many miles do two inches stand for?

Step 3 It is about five inches on the map from Pittsburgh to Plymouth. So the distance from the real city of Pittsburgh to Plymouth must be about 500 miles.

Practice the Skill

Look at the map. Follow the directions to find distances. Use a ruler.

1 About how many inches is it on the map from Plymouth to Washington, D.C.?

2 How many miles is it from Plymouth to Washington, D.C.? Use the scale to find out.

3 A truck carries clams from Plymouth to Ithaca. How many miles does the truck travel?

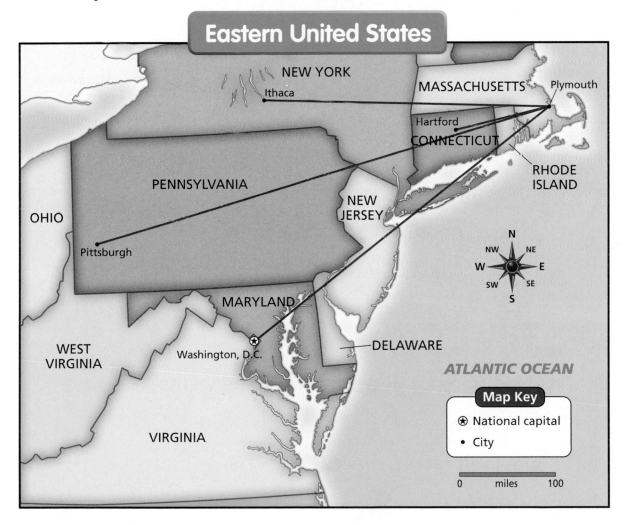

Eastern United States

Big Ideas

Producers and Consumers

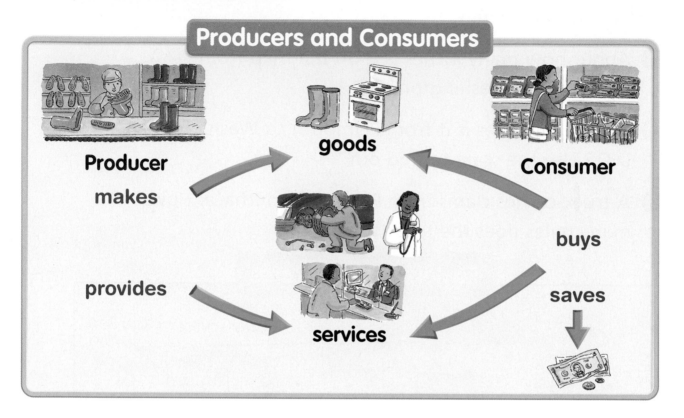

Producer
makes → goods
provides → services

Consumer
goods ← buys
services ← saves

Choose the missing words from the organizer.

1. A _____ makes goods.   2. A consumer buys _____ and services.   3. A consumer may _____ money in a bank.

STANDARDS **1.** HSS 2.4.2 **2.** HSS 2.4.2 **3.** HSS 2.4

Facts and Main Ideas

4. What is the difference between needs and wants? (page 160)

5. What is income? (page 168)

6. What is one job that is a service? (page 173)

7. What does **scarcity** mean? (page 192)

4. HSS 2.4 **5.** HSS 2.4 **6.** HSS 2.4.2 **7.** HSS 2.4.3

Vocabulary

Use words from the box to complete the sentences.

Consumers earn **8.** _____
to pay for needs and **9.** _____ .
One need is **10.** _____ .
Consumers look at the
11. _____ of goods and
12. _____ . Consumers may
save money in a **13.** _____
to pay later for things they want.

8. HSS 2.4 **9.** HSS 2.4.3 **10.** HSS 2.4 **11.** HSS 2.4.2
12. HSS 2.4.2 **13.** HSS 2.4 **14.** HSS 2.4

A. prices (page 180)

B. income (page 168)

C. savings account
(page 182)

D. services (page 173)

E. specialize (page 199)

F. wants (page 160)

G. shelter (page 160)

 Test Practice

14. What does the word **barter** mean?

    A. earning a small income

    B. saving money in a bank

    C. trading without money

    D. producing many goods

Critical Thinking

Main Idea and Details

15. What are two examples of human resources?

16. What are two examples of trade?

15. HSS 2.4 **16.** HSS 2.3.2

Review

Skillbuilders **Use a Map Scale**

17. On this map, one inch equals _____ .

18. How far is it from Maria's house to the airport?

17. Analysis Skill CST 4 18. Analysis Skill CST 4

Read a Bar Graph

19. Which place at school has the fewest workers?

20. How many workers are in the office and the cafeteria all together?

19. Analysis Skill HI 2 20. Analysis Skill HI 2

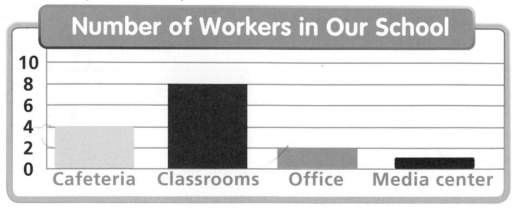

Unit Activity

The Big Idea

Make a Mobile

If you earned $10, how much of your money would you spend and save?

❶ Write and draw your choices.

❷ Make sure that they add up to $10.

❸ Cut out your choices and hang them up to make a mobile. Explain your choices.

Save $2.00 in bank

Spend $4.00 on cat toy

Spend $4.00 on colored pencils

Current Events

Current Events Project

Find articles about jobs around the world. Publish a **Class Newspaper** about people at work around the world.

JOBS AROUND THE WORLD

Rug weaving   Fishing

Technology

Read articles about current events at **www.eduplace.com/kids/hmss/**

In Your Classroom

Look for these Social Studies Independent Books in your classroom.

At the Library

You may find these books at your school or public library.

Follow the Money
by Loreen Leedy

The Paperboy
by Dav Pilkey

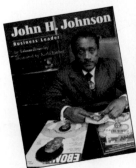

UNIT 5

America's Past

"Let Freedom ring."

Samuel Francis Smith,
from the song "America," 1831

The Big Idea

Why is the past important to you today?

Vocabulary Preview

Technology
e • glossary
e • word games
www.eduplace.com/kids/hmss/

explorer

We remember Christopher Columbus, an **explorer** who traveled to find new things and places. page 222

colonist

A **colonist** is a person who lives in a colony. Many colonists came to America seeking freedom. page 230

Reading Strategy

Use the **predict and infer** reading strategy in Lessons 1, 2, 3, and 4 and the **monitor and clarify** strategy in Lessons 5, 6, and 7.

independence

The 13 colonies gained independence from Great Britain. **Independence** is freedom from the rule of another nation. page 242

technology

Technology is the use of science to make new things or to make things work better. page 260

First Americans

▶ **Vocabulary**

history

◎ **Reading Skill**

Classify

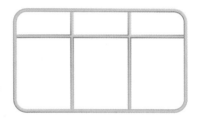

⬛ **STANDARDS**

Core: HSS 2.1, Analysis Skill CST 2, HI 1
Extend support: Analysis Skill CST 3

Build on What You Know How old are you? Your age now is in the present. You will be a grownup in the future. You were a baby in the past.

History

You remember things that happened in the past. Also you learn about the past from family stories. **History** is everything we can know about the past. History is everything that happened in the lives of people from far back in the past up to the present.

main (★) *idea*

A storyteller in Alaska uses his drum to tell a traditional tale to young people.

The First People in America

Our country's history starts with American 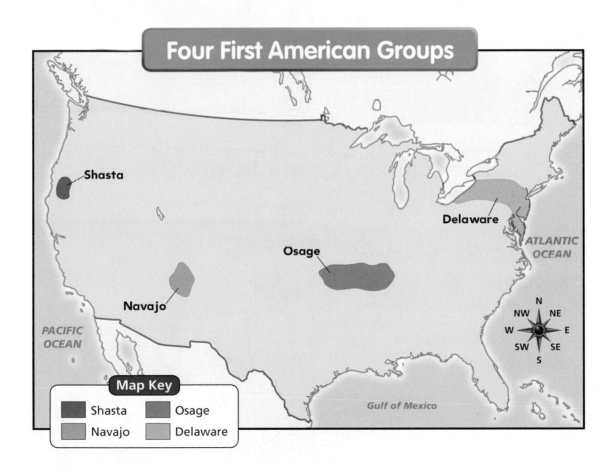 Indians. Hundreds of American Indian groups already lived in America more than 500 years ago. They depended on natural resources. American Indians used water, land, and plants in many different ways. Their clothes, tools, and other things from the past help us learn about their lives.

This map locates just four of the many groups of American Indians. They are the four you will learn about on the next pages.

Four First American Groups

Shasta

Delaware

ATLANTIC OCEAN

Osage

Navajo

PACIFIC OCEAN

N
NW NE
W   E
SW SE
S

Gulf of Mexico

Map Key
Shasta   Osage
Navajo   Delaware

Skill **Reading Maps** Which group was in the northwest?

Compare Groups

The Delaware, Living in Woodlands

Homes winter longhouse for several families; summer wigwam for each family
Clothes made from deerskin
Food nuts, berries, corn, beans, squash, deer meat
Travel by canoe, on foot

The Navajo, Living in the Desert

Home hogan
Clothes made from animal skins, plants
Food cactus fruit, wild potatoes, corn, beans, squash, antelope and deer meat
Travel on foot

The Osage, Living on the Plains

Homes winter longhouses for several families, small summer homes for travelers
Clothes made from deerskin
Food nuts, plums, grapes, potatoes, corn, beans, pumpkins, turkey, buffalo
Travel on foot, by canoe

The Shasta, Living Near the Ocean

Homes winter dwelling house for several families, summer cool brush shelter
Clothes made from animal skins, fur, braided grass
Food bulbs, berries, pine nuts, acorns, turtles, grasshoppers, fish, deer, elk
Travel on foot, with snowshoes in winter, by canoe

Natural Resources and Daily Life

These pictures show some things that American Indians made and used hundreds of years ago. People in the present might see these things in a museum. American Indians used many natural resources to make the things they needed. (★) main idea

Navajo sandals were made from braided leaves of desert plants.

The Osage and other groups who lived on the plains wove baskets from long grasses.

Some American Indian groups in plains and woodlands made dugout canoes from logs of trees.

Review Where might people today see things that people made hundreds of years ago?

Lesson Review

❶ **Vocabulary** Write a sentence that uses the words **history** and **American Indian**.

❷ **Main Idea** Why were natural resources important to American Indians?

✏ **Activity** Choose two groups and tell a way they were alike and a way they were different.

The Young Woman and the Thunder Beings

This legend is retold by Joseph Bruchac in his book Between Earth and Sky. In the past, the Seneca told this story. In the present they still tell it. Read it to see why.

To the North lived the Longhouse People, near the edge of the falls called Ne-ah-ga.

They sometimes spoke of the Thunder Beings who lived in a cave beneath the falls. When a child wanted to give thanks to the Thunderers for the gift of rain, he would place an offering in a canoe and put it in the river to float over the falls.

One day a young woman alone in her canoe was crossing the river far up from the falls when she lost her paddle. The current was swift and she found herself swept away. This brave young woman had always been a friend of the Thunderers, giving them gifts with each new season. So, as she fell, she did not scream or cry. In trust, she asked calmly for help.

The Thunder Beings saved her life, catching her safely in their blanket. Then the chief of the Thunderers asked the young woman to be his wife. She agreed, and to this day, the Seneca say that when the rumbling voices of the Thunder Beings roll across the sky, the brave young woman is keeping watch, reminding us that every gift we give gives us back a blessing.

Activities

1. **Talk About It** Why did the Thunder Beings save the girl?

2. **Act It Out** List the characters in the story and act out what they do.

Explorers Travel the World

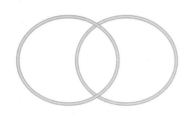
Build on What You Know Have you traveled to a place that was new to you? What did you learn about it?

Explorers from Europe

An **explorer** is a person who travels to find out new things. A **journey** is a trip. Many hundreds of years ago, explorers from Europe traveled to other lands. They did not have cars, planes, or steam engines then. Their maps did not show much about the places they were going. Their journeys were filled with adventures.

Marco Polo

Marco Polo

More than 700 years ago, a man from Italy named Marco Polo traveled to Asia. He spent many years in China. He told thrilling stories about new things he saw on his journeys. His stories were put into a book. Most people in Europe knew nothing about what Asia was like. Marco Polo's stories made them want to find out more.

Marco Polo in the court of the Chinese emperor

Review Why was Marco Polo important in history?

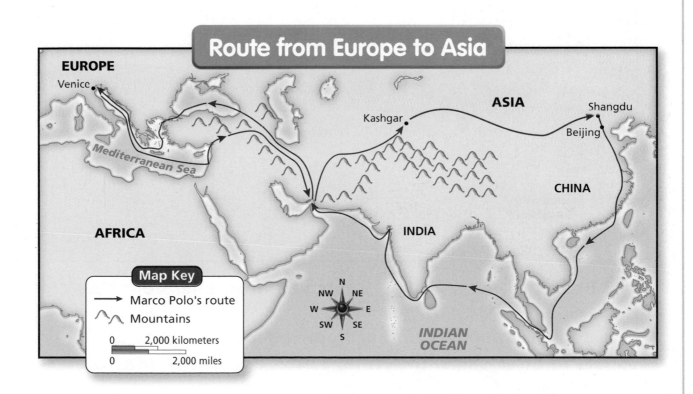

Route from Europe to Asia

EUROPE
Venice

Mediterranean Sea

AFRICA

ASIA

Kashgar

Shangdu

Beijing

CHINA

INDIA

Map Key
→ Marco Polo's route
⋀⋀ Mountains

0   2,000 kilometers
0   2,000 miles

N
NW   NE
W   E
SW   SE
S

INDIAN OCEAN

Christopher Columbus

Christopher Columbus was an explorer from Europe who wanted to find a faster way to reach parts of Asia. Columbus read Marco Polo's stories and studied many maps. He decided to sail west across the Atlantic Ocean. His ships reached land that he thought was Asia. Explorers who came later learned that it was not Asia. It was another continent—now called North America.

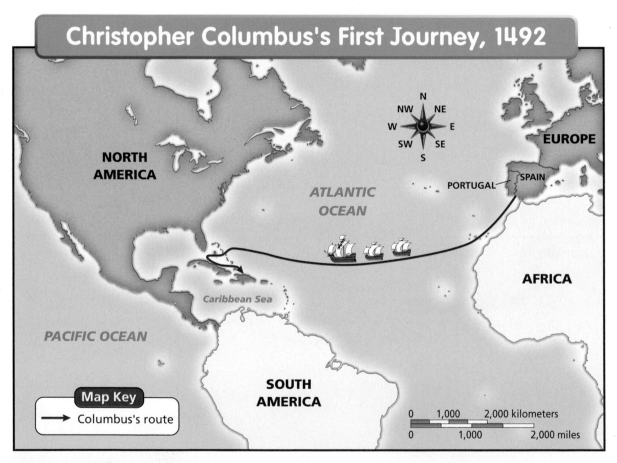

Christopher Columbus's First Journey, 1492

NORTH AMERICA

EUROPE

PORTUGAL

SPAIN

ATLANTIC OCEAN

AFRICA

Caribbean Sea

PACIFIC OCEAN

SOUTH AMERICA

Map Key
→ Columbus's route

0   1,000   2,000 kilometers
0   1,000   2,000 miles

Skill **Reading Maps** What ocean did Christopher Columbus cross?

Christopher Columbus set out from Spain with a crew of ninety sailors in three ships, the **Niña**, **Pinta**, and **Santa Maria**.

The journeys of Christopher Columbus changed what people knew about the world. North America and South America soon became part of the world map for Europeans. The new knowledge led to other changes for people who lived in the Americas.

Christopher Columbus

Review Why did Christopher Columbus sail west?

Lesson Review

1 **Vocabulary** Write a sentence that uses the words **journey** and **explorer.**

2 **Main Idea** Why was Marco Polo's journey important to Christopher Columbus?

Activity Write or tell a way that Marco Polo and Christopher Columbus were alike and a way they were different.

1. HSS 2.1 **2.** HSS 2.1 **Activity** HSS 2.1

The Magnetic Compass

How did Christopher Columbus find his way across the Atlantic Ocean? A magnetic compass helped him.

A magnetic compass is like a compass rose. It shows directions: north, south, east and west. But a magnetic compass has something more. It has a needle that is a magnet. Because the needle is a magnet, it always points towards the earth's North Pole. Once you know where north is, you can find east, south, and west too.

People in China were the first to make magnetic compasses.

Read a Magnetic Compass

1 Rest the compass on a table. Find the colored end of the needle. That end points north.

2 Locate the letters N, E, S, and W. Name the direction word that each letter stands for.

3 Gently turn the compass until the needle is in line with the letter N. What does the needle do when you turn the compass?

4 Hold both arms out together ahead of you and face the direction that the compass points. You should be facing and pointing north.

Jamestown and Plymouth

Vocabulary
colony
settlement
colonist
Pilgrim

Reading Skill
Compare and Contrast

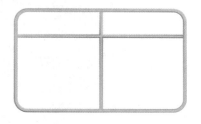

STANDARDS
Core: HSS 2.1, 2.3.2, 2.4, Analysis Skill HI 1, HI 4
Extend support: HSS 2.1

Build on What You Know How would you feel about moving to a place far away?

American Land

After Columbus, more explorers from Europe traveled to other parts of North America. They hoped to find gold and other riches. They saw great natural resources in the forests, plains, and rivers. American Indians already lived there. But kings and queens from countries in Europe wanted the land for their countries. They sent people to settle in North America.

English Colonies

A **colony** is a place that is ruled by another country. England was one of the countries that started colonies in North America. People from England traveled in ships to settle there. Their colonies began with small communities called **settlements.** The map shows two of the earliest settlements. See what you can learn about Plymouth and Jamestown from the map.

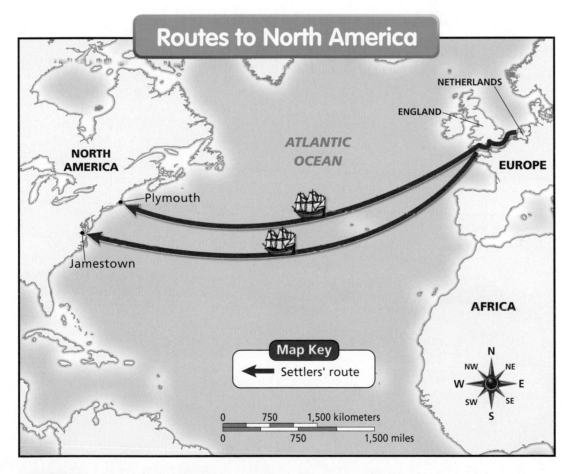

Routes to North America

NETHERLANDS

ENGLAND

NORTH AMERICA

ATLANTIC OCEAN

EUROPE

Plymouth

Jamestown

AFRICA

Map Key

← Settlers' route

N
NW   NE
W   E
SW   SE
S

0   750   1,500 kilometers
0   750   1,500 miles

Skill **Reading Maps** Why do you think both settlements were built near water?

Jamestown

A **colonist** is a person who lives in a colony. The first colonists in Jamestown were men and boys. They worked hard to stay alive. The colonists cut down trees, which they used to build a fort and some houses.

At first they did not have enough food. They ate fish and turtles, even raccoons. Nearby American Indians called the Pamunkey gave them some corn. Also, the colonists had copper that they traded for corn. The Pamunkey wanted the copper to make jewelry.

Later the colonists sent for others in their families. Life was hard for everyone. Children worked along with grownups.

Soon the colonists at Jamestown began to produce goods, such as lumber and window glass. They sent these products to be sold in England.

Skill **Visual Learning** What are some things in the picture that show what colonists in Jamestown did?

Plymouth

Many of the first colonists at Plymouth belonged to the same religious group. They became known as **Pilgrims.** The Pilgrims came to America because they wanted freedom to follow their religious beliefs. Whole families came together. In the first year, they faced sickness, fire, and freezing weather. American Indians called the Wampanoag (wahm puh NOH ag) helped the Pilgrims. The Wampanoag showed the Pilgrims how to plant, hunt, and fish.

Everyone had to help out. Girls and boys helped cook, clean, and look after the younger children. Women kept the gardens. They made and mended the family's clothes. They taught the children to read and write. Men built homes. They hunted and fished and planted corn.

Review In what ways was daily life in Plymouth like daily life in Jamestown?

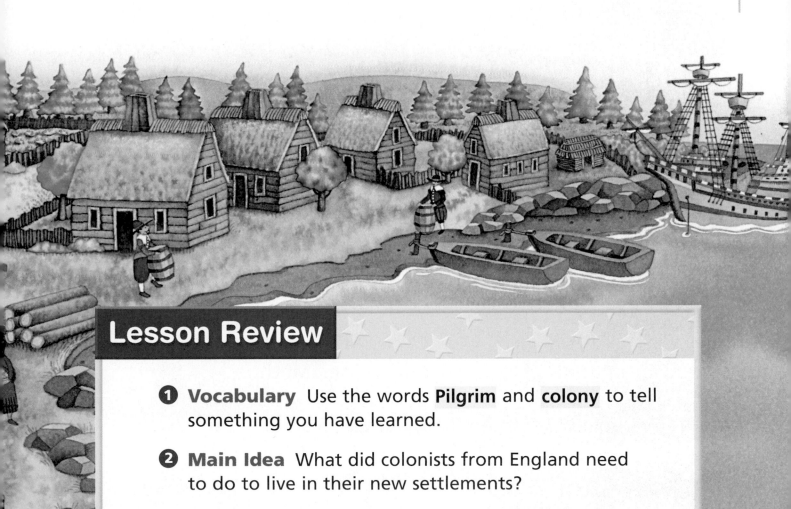

Lesson Review

1 Vocabulary Use the words **Pilgrim** and **colony** to tell something you have learned.

2 Main Idea What did colonists from England need to do to live in their new settlements?

Activity Write a letter to a friend. Tell what you found out about life in Jamestown and Plymouth.

The Mayflower Crossing

What was the ocean crossing like for the Pilgrims aboard the **Mayflower**? Follow them on their journey from England to America.

Characters

Narrator

Mary Brewster: woman

Love Brewster: Mary's son

Constance Hopkins: girl

William Bradford: man

Rose Standish: woman

Elizabeth Tilley: girl

Thomas English: sailor

Scene 1

Narrator: It is September 10, 1620. The **Mayflower** has been at sea for four days.

Love: I am so tired of looking at the ocean, Mother.

Mary: Be patient. There are many days ahead on this little ship.

Thomas: Better go below! A storm is coming! You will find it a little too exciting on deck!

Scene 2

Narrator: Two weeks pass. The sea grows rougher.

Constance: I wish this awful rolling would stop!

Rose: If we only had fresh water.

Love: Or a hot meal. Even beans would do.

Mary: Be glad we have cheese and biscuits.

Elizabeth: Father says the main beam of the ship has cracked.

William: Don't worry. The sailors are fixing it.

Thomas: We'll use these tools to pull the beam together.

Scene 3

Narrator: Halfway through the crossing, during a storm, a cry goes up.

Thomas: Help! John Howland has washed overboard!

Elizabeth: He fell from the main deck!

Love: Wait! He has grabbed hold of a rope.

Elizabeth: They are lifting him out! He is safe, thank goodness.

William: Listen. There is another cry: a new-born baby!

Constance: Mother has had a baby boy. She has named him Oceanus. They are both doing well.

All: Congratulations!

William: This news should give us all hope.

Scene 4

Narrator: In November, more than nine weeks after leaving England, we hear the call we've been waiting for.

Thomas: Land!

Elizabeth: I see it! A long curving beach.

Rose: My husband, Miles, will bring men ashore.

William: We will look for a good place to build our community.

Love: Fresh water!

Rose and Mary: Clean clothes!

William: Friends, it is time to begin our new lives.

Activities

1. **Think About It** What do you think was most difficult for the passengers of the **Mayflower?**

2. **Write About It** Write a letter you might have sent to England if you had sailed on the **Mayflower.**

Identify Cause and Effect

▶ **Vocabulary**

cause

effect

The Pilgrims wanted to land at the Hudson River. They thought the river was part of Virginia. Why did they land on Cape Cod? Knowing about cause and effect can help you understand what happened.

Learn the Skill

A **cause** makes something happen. Something that happens is an **effect.**

Step 1 Look at this map. The star shows the place the Pilgrims wanted to land. The dots show where the Pilgrims really landed.

Step 2 Use the map to find one thing that caused the **Mayflower** to change its route. The map shows that one cause was a storm.

Step 3 You can explain cause and effect using the word **because.** The **Mayflower** changed its route because it hit a storm.

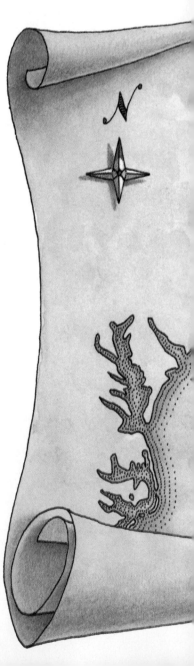

Practice the Skill

STANDARDS Analysis Skill HI 3, CST 4, 5

Follow the directions to identify cause and effect.

1 The storm forced the **Mayflower** north of its planned route. When it got near land, the ship started south. What caused the ship to turn back?

2 What are two causes for why the Pilgrims landed on Cape Cod?

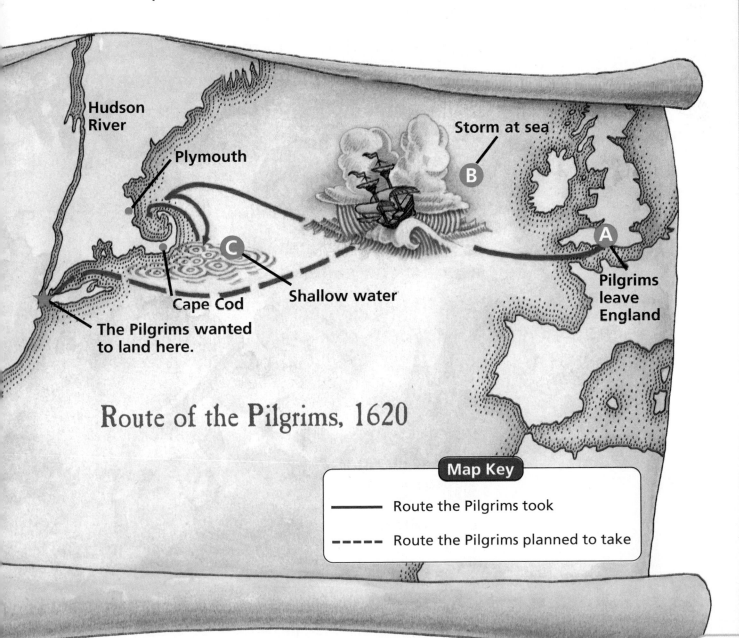

Hudson River

Plymouth

Storm at sea

B

A

C

Shallow water

Cape Cod

The Pilgrims wanted to land here.

Pilgrims leave England

Route of the Pilgrims, 1620

Map Key

——— Route the Pilgrims took

- - - - - Route the Pilgrims planned to take

People from America's Past

Vocabulary

independence

Reading Skill

Sequence

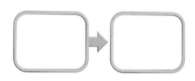

STANDARDS

Core: HSS 2.3.2, 2.5, Analysis Skill HI 1
Extend support: HSS 2.5

Build on What You Know Have you had to follow rules that didn't seem fair to you?

Many Colonies

After the first settlements in Jamestown and Plymouth, more people came from England to settle in North America. They built homes and churches. They started farms and businesses. Some small communities grew into large towns and cities. People worked and planned together. But they had to follow rules from the king of England, who was the ruler of Great Britain and its colonies.

The map shows thirteen of the colonies in North America in 1763.

Review What were the names of the colonies?

The Thirteen Colonies

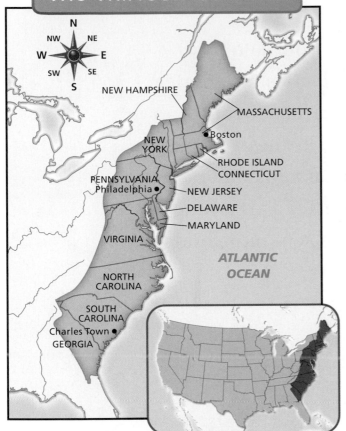

NEW HAMPSHIRE

MASSACHUSETTS

Boston

NEW YORK

RHODE ISLAND
CONNECTICUT

PENNSYLVANIA
Philadelphia

NEW JERSEY

DELAWARE

MARYLAND

VIRGINIA

ATLANTIC OCEAN

NORTH CAROLINA

SOUTH CAROLINA

Charles Town

GEORGIA

Boston 3

Charles Town 3

Philadelphia 3

Independence

Independence means being free from rule by another nation. More and more colonists in America wanted independence from Great Britain. Some colonists began to act against British rules and taxes. One group of colonists acted against a tax on tea. Their action was called the Boston Tea Party. King George ruled Great Britain then. He sent more and more armies to control the colonists.

Look at events on the timeline.

main ★ idea

December 1773
Boston Tea Party

April 1775
British army fights with colonists in Massachusetts

1770   1773   1775

The Declaration of Independence

People from the thirteen colonies did not all agree about independence from Great Britain. Each colony sent people to Philadelphia to meet and make a decision. People at the meeting chose Thomas Jefferson to write words explaining why the colonies wanted independence. Those words became the Declaration of Independence. By signing the Declaration of Independence, colonists came together for the goal of independence.

main idea (★)

Review What did colonists do that showed they wanted independence?

July 1776
Thirteen colonies agree on the Declaration of Independence

1776

1780

This painting shows an artist's idea of how George Washington looked when he crossed the Delaware River during the American Revolution.

The American Revolution

Great Britain would not allow independence. King George sent soldiers to fight a war against the colonists. The war was called the American Revolution. George Washington led the soldiers who fought against Britain. There were terrible battles. The American Revolution lasted eight years. Finally in 1783, the war ended. The colonies had won independence. They became a country called the United States of America.

main (★) *idea*

Leaders for Independence

You have read how George Washington and Thomas Jefferson helped America gain independence. Many others helped too. **Benjamin Franklin** got colonists to think and talk about why they wanted independence. **Abigail Adams** wrote what she saw and thought about the fight for independence. **Samuel Adams** made speeches that got many colonists to fight for independence. **Paul Revere** helped colonists work together against Great Britain.

Benjamin Franklin

Samuel Adams

Review Why did colonists fight in the American Revolution?

Lesson Review

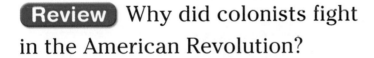

1 **Vocabulary** Use the word **independence** in a sentence about colonists.

2 **Main Idea** Why was the Declaration of Independence important to the colonists?

HANDS ON

Activity Draw a picture of a person or an event that helped America become an independent country. Tell why that person or event was important.

1. HSS 2.3.2 **2.** HSS 2.3.2 **Activity** HSS 2.5

Two Patriots

Abigail Adams and Paul Revere both used their minds and hands to help win independence for their country.

Abigail Adams

Abigail Adams always loved to write long letters. She described events in exciting detail and shared her own ideas.

Abigail married John Adams, who was a leader in the American Revolution. He often traveled far from home. Abigail wrote to him daily. She described life with their children and troubles from the war. Abigail also explained her own ideas about **independence**.

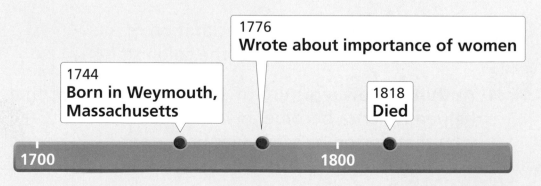

1776
Wrote about importance of women

1744
Born in Weymouth, Massachusetts

1818
Died

1700

1800

In this letter, Abigail Adams told John to "remember the ladies..." in the fight for independence.

Paul Revere

Paul Revere boldly joined other colonists who showed they were against British rule. He kept on doing many things to fight for independence.

At night on April 18, 1775, Paul Revere rode his horse from Boston to warn colonists of a British army plan. This prepared colonists in Lexington to fight a battle that became known as the start of the American Revolution. His brave ride became famous in a poem by Henry Wadsworth Longfellow.

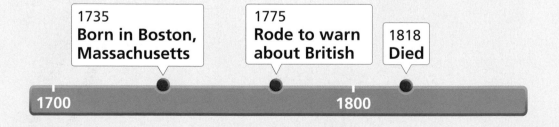

1735
Born in Boston, Massachusetts

1775
Rode to warn about British

1818
Died

1700

1800

A picture book of Longfellow's poem

Activities

1. **Write About It** Write or tell two ways that Paul Revere and Abigail Adams showed **patriotism.**

2. **Make It** Make a poster that shows something important about the life of Abigail Adams or Paul Revere.

Compare Fact and Opinion

▶ **Vocabulary**

fact

opinion

A **fact** is something that is true. An **opinion** is what someone thinks. Two people can have different opinions about the same facts.

Learn the Skill

Step 1 Read the sentences about Independence Day. One sentence tells a fact. The other sentence tells an opinion.

> Independence Day is on July 4 every year.

> I think Independence Day is the best national holiday.

Step 2 A fact is something that is true. You can check to see if a fact is true. A fact is probably true if two or more good nonfiction books agree.

Step 3 Opinions use words such as "I think."

Practice the Skill

STANDARDS HSS 2.5

Read the sentences. Then follow the directions.

1 In what way is a fact different from an opinion?

2 Which sentences below tell facts?

3 Which sentence below tells an opinion? Tell how you know that it is an opinion.

George Washington was the first President of our country.

John Hancock's signature is the largest on the Declaration of Independence.

I think Benjamin Franklin was the greatest inventor of all time.

Past Heroes

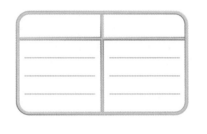
Build on What You Know Think of a person who is special.

Heroes

A **hero** is someone who does something brave for the good of others or works hard to help others. Some heroes are strong leaders of a group. Some heroes are inventors. An inventor is someone who finds new ways to do things. Look at some heroes from the past. They were important to people in the past, and they are still important today.

Charles Drew made the model for ways to collect and store blood for patients.

★ Sitting Bull ★

Sitting Bull was a leader of the Lakota nation. He was known for being powerful, brave, and wise. He believed strongly in Lakota traditions. (★) main idea

Sitting Bull was against the United States control of Lakota land. He helped the Lakota nation to fight the United States Army. He always stood firmly for a way of life he felt was right.

Sitting Bull

Lakota Homelands

Review Why is Sitting Bull still a hero?

★ Golda Meir ★

Golda Meir was a Jewish immigrant from Russia to the United States. As a young woman, she joined others who worked to start a Jewish nation called Israel. Golda Meir gave strong speeches. She worked hard to start the new nation. <u>Golda Meir was a leader of Israel.</u> She was one of the first women to lead a country.

main idea (★)

ISRAEL

Golda Meir

★ Jackie Robinson ★

Jackie Robinson was excellent in many sports. In 1947, he became the first African American baseball player in the National League. At that time, many people did not want African American players to be with white players. They did hurtful things to make him quit. But Jackie Robinson did not quit. He kept playing baseball. He set a great example. Other African American players began to join teams with white players.

Jackie Robinson

Review What are some ways that Jackie Robinson, Golda Meir, and Sitting Bull are alike?

★ Thomas Edison ★

Thomas Edison was a great inventor.  Even as a boy, he loved to try out new ideas. He learned science on his own. In his life, he produced more than a thousand inventions. An **invention** is something new that someone makes or thinks of. Two of Thomas Edison's inventions were the electric light bulb and sound recordings. These inventions changed people's daily lives.

Thomas Edison

★ Albert Einstein ★

Albert Einstein grew up in Germany. As a young child, he was excited by science questions. As an adult, Albert Einstein kept thinking about science. He explained how light works. He changed ideas in science about time and space. His work helped people understand the world.

main (★) idea

Review What is a way that Albert Einstein and Thomas Edison are alike?

Albert Einstein

Lesson Review

❶ **Vocabulary** Write a sentence that tells why one of the people you have read about is a **hero.**

❷ **Main Idea** Why are heroes from the past still important to people today?

✏ **Activity** Write a summary that tells why Thomas Edison was an important inventor.

1. HSS 2.5 2. HSS 2.5 **Activity** HSS 2.5

257

LEARN FROM A LETTER

Do you like to save letters or cards from people you know? Branch Rickey saved a thank-you letter from Jackie Robinson. Now, more than fifty years later, we can learn from it.

Branch Rickey was the manager of the Brooklyn Dodgers baseball team. When he hired Jackie Robinson for the Dodgers, some people said that the team was headed for big trouble. Jackie Robinson wrote this letter after three years of great playing for the Dodgers. He wrote because Branch Rickey was leaving the team.

HOTEL *Jaragua*

CIUDAD TRUJILLO • REPUBLICA DOMINICANA

. . . It has been the finest experience I have had being associated [a friend] with you and I want to thank you very much for all you have meant not only to me and my family but to the entire country and particularly [mostly to] members of our race. . . .

My wife joins me in saying thanks very much Mr. Rickey. . .

Sincerely yours,

Jackie Robinson

Activities

1. **Talk About It** What did Branch Rickey do to show respect for Jackie Robinson?

2. **Write About It** Name someone you would like to thank. Write a letter to the person with your reasons for thanking him or her.

Communities Change

Vocabulary

transportation
technology

Reading Skill

Sequence

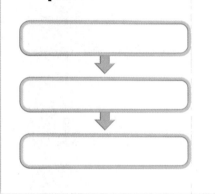

STANDARDS

Core: HSS 2.1, 2.2, 2.5, Analysis Skill CST 1, 3, 4, 5
Extend support: HSS 2.5, Analysis Skill CST 3

Build on What You Know What are some ways that you have traveled? Do you think those ways were possible for people two hundred years ago?

Transportation

Transportation is any way of moving things or people from one place to another. When people travel or move goods, they use transportation.

Technology is using science to make things work better. Inventors have used technology to make transportation faster, stronger, and safer. Technology has helped them make new kinds of transportation. New kinds of transportation have changed how people live in a community.

main idea (★)

The two maps show changes in one community: Plainfield, Illinois. Compare the roads on both maps.

Illinois

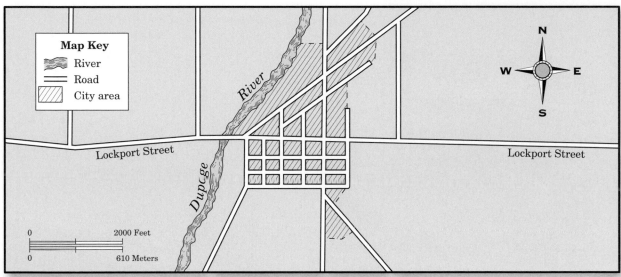

Plainfield, Illinois, more than 100 years ago

Plainfield today

Review What is a way that technology has changed communities?

Transportation Changes Plainfield

Look at some changes in transportation that brought more people and business to this community.

1850   1900

1834

People came by stagecoach to settle in the new town. Stagecoaches also brought travelers who stopped for food and rest.

1904

People rode streetcars on railways between towns. Many came to Plainfield for vacations in a place called Electric Park.

1920

The first paved highway to cross the country went through Plainfield. Cars and buses brought more people. Trucks brought goods quickly. More businesses opened.

Review What were three kinds of transportation that went through Plainfield?

2000

2004

Now many highways go around and through Plainfield. It is a suburb of Chicago. People have built more homes and schools. Families keep moving to Plainfield.

Lesson Review

❶ **Vocabulary** Tell a way that technology has changed transportation.

❷ **Main Idea** Give an example of how transportation changed Plainfield.

✏ **Activity** Name a kind of transportation that people use today. Explain how it helps people.

Two Inventors

Both inventors found new ways to do things in transportation.

Granville T. Woods

Train crashes were a big problem when Granville T. Woods was a young man. He invented a Railway Telegraph that located moving trains. It kept trains from crashing. Granville T. Woods invented much more. He invented a grooved wheel that allowed a street car, or trolley, to receive electricity to move it along tracks. Granville T. Woods started a company to make and sell his inventions.

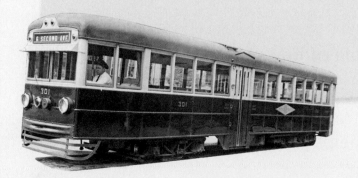

Taylor G. Wang

Taylor Wang is a scientist, an inventor, and a college teacher. He wanted to find new ways for scientists to work in space. To do this he became an astronaut. He set up a science lab on the space shuttle. During the flight he was always solving problems in the lab. Taylor Wang and other scientists still use what he learned in space.

Activities

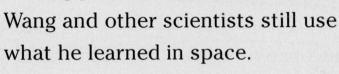

1. **Act It Out** Act out or describe something Granville T. Woods or Taylor Wang did as an inventor.

2. **List It** Make a list of facts about Granville T. Woods and another list of facts about Taylor G. Wang. Use the lists to compare the two inventors.

Understand Point of View

▶ **Vocabulary**

point of view

A **point of view** is what someone thinks about something. When people give reasons for what they think, they help others understand their point of view.

Learn the Skill

Step 1 Read this question. **What do you think was the best invention in transportation? Tell why.**

Step 2 Read two different points of view.

- **Jeff:** I think the railroad train was best, because more people could travel across land after that.
- **Sheera:** I think the airplane was the best invention. Flying helped people get places much faster.

Step 3 Both Jeff and Sheera gave reasons for their points of view. Tell two ways their points of view are different.

STANDARDS Analysis Skill REPV 2

Practice the Skill

1 Look at the pictures of inventions in transportation below. Which do you think was the best invention?

2 Give your answer. Make sure to tell a reason for your point of view.

3 Tell a way that your point of view is different from Jeff's or Sheera's or the point of view of someone in your class.

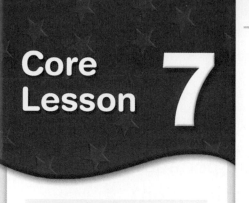

Communication Changes

▶ **Vocabulary**

communication

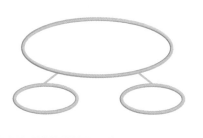**Reading Skill**

Main Idea and Details

🔖 **STANDARDS**

Core: HSS 2.1, Analysis Skill CST 3
Extend support: HSS 2.1, Analysis Skill CST 3

Build on What You Know What are some ways that you can leave a message for someone? Which of those ways were possible 200 years ago?

Communication in History

Communication is any way of sharing information. Communication has (★) changed over the years.

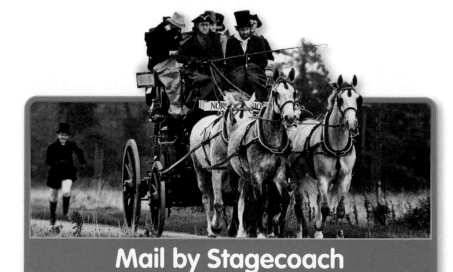

Mail by Stagecoach

In 1776, Benjamin Franklin headed the American postal system. He got stagecoaches to carry mail between post offices. This helped letters reach people faster.

Telegraph

In 1844, an American, Samuel Morse, invented a telegraph system. People could then send messages along a wire. They used a code of clicks to stand for letters of the alphabet. They could send news quickly along hundreds of miles of wire..

Telephone

In 1876, Alexander Graham Bell showed how people could send voice messages along a wire. These were the first telephones. Once telephone wires were strung across the country, people could talk even if they lived far apart.

Review In what way were the telegraph system and postal system alike?

Radio

By 1900, inventors had used technology to send messages by airwaves. This led to the radio. Over time, people began to have radios at home. Families around the country could listen to the same music, news, or speeches. People heard plays, comedies, and stories too.

Television

In the 1920s and 1930s, inventors showed how people could see events live on television. Then some inventors found ways to make it work well in homes. By the 1950's many families had television.

Internet

By 1975, inventors had ways to connect computers. They called these networks. People could send messages between computers in a network. Soon computers around the world could join one huge network called the Internet. What can you do on the Internet?

Review In what ways are radio and television alike?

Lesson Review

1 **Vocabulary** Use the word **communication** in a sentence about something you use now.

2 **Main Idea** Give two examples of something that changed communication after 1775.

 Activity Ask a parent, grandparent, or guardian how people traveled when they were children. On a poster, show the differences and similarities between travel then and today.

Runners with a Message

Long ago in South America people called the Incas got messages from runners. The runners were young men who trained to run very fast. They had to learn to remember every word of the message. They had to speak it very clearly. One runner started with a message. He ran for miles along a road to a spot where another runner waited. Each runner had to listen closely and then run on with the message. What could happen if one runner did not listen well?

Inca pots had paintings of Inca runners.

Inca
Lands

Activities

1. Act It Out Try sending a message as Inca runners did.

2. Write It Write a message to a friend. Use complete sentences.

Big Ideas

The Big Idea

Timeline in American History

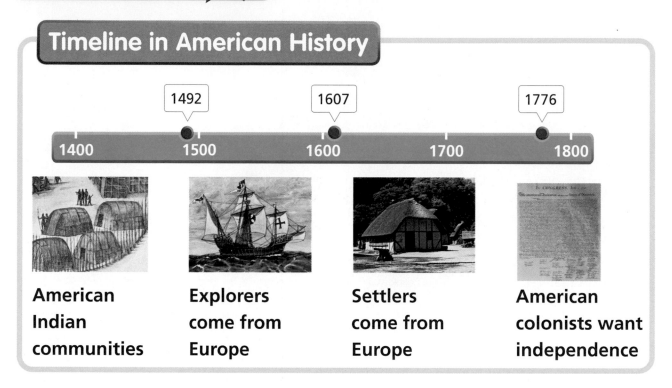

| 1492 | 1607 | 1776 |

1400   1500   1600   1700   1800

American Indian communities

Explorers come from Europe

Settlers come from Europe

American colonists want independence

Find the missing words on the timeline.

1. _____ lived in America before explorers came.

2. _____ came after explorers from Europe.

3. In 1776, _____ said they wanted independence.

STANDARDS **1.** Analysis Skill HI 1 **2.** Analysis Skill HI 1 **3.** HSS 2.3.2

Facts and Main Ideas

4. What was a food that American Indians ate? (pages 214, 215)

5. Name two kinds of work the Plymouth colonists did. (pages 232, 233)

6. Name two leaders who wanted independence from Great Britain. (pages 243, 244, 245)

7. Who were two American inventors? (pages 256, 257, 264, 265)

4. HSS 2.1 **5.** HSS 2.4 **6.** HSS 2.5 **7.** HSS 2.5

Vocabulary

Choose the letter of the word that best matches the picture.

8.

9.

10.

11.

12.

A. **explorer** (page 222)

B. **colonist** (page 230)

C. **settlement** (page 229)

D. **communication** (page 268)

E. **transportation** (page 260)

8. HSS 2.1 9. HSS 2.1 10. HSS 2.1 11. HSS 2.1 12. HSS 2.1 13. HSS 2.1

 Test Practice

13. What does the word **history** mean?

   A. a long trip
   B. a Plymouth colonist
   C. everything you can know about the past
   D. new things people make or think of

Critical Thinking

Sequence

14. Who came first? Who came next? List these people in time order.

   a. Christopher Columbus   b. Marco Polo   c. Thomas Jefferson

14. Analysis Skill CST 1

Review

Identify Cause and Effect

Read the paragraph and answer the questions.

When colonists in America wanted independence, the king of England sent the British army to control them. More colonists became angry at the actions of the king. They decided to fight for independence.

The Beginning of the American Revolution

15. Why did the king of England send armies to America?

16. Why did the colonists fight the British army?

15. Analysis Skill HI 3 16. Analysis Skill HI 3

Compare Fact and Opinion

A fact is something that is true. An opinion is what someone thinks.

17. Which sentence tells a fact?

18. Which sentence is an opinion? Tell if you agree or disagree.

17. Analysis Skill REPV 3 18. Analysis Skill REPV 3

A. I think it would be fun to sail on the **Mayflower.**

B. The **Mayflower** landed in America in 1620.

Unit Activity

The Big Idea

Make a History Puppet

Choose a person from American history and make a puppet of that person.

1 Make the puppet's head and costume.

2 Write three questions that you would like people to ask your puppet.

3 Use your hand and voice so that your puppet answers the questions.

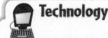

Current Events

What events are taking place in your area? Make an **Events in the News Timeline.**

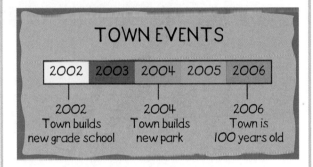

TOWN EVENTS

| 2002 | 2003 | 2004 | 2005 | 2006 |

2002
Town builds
new grade school

2004
Town builds
new park

2006
Town is
100 years old

Technology

Read articles about current events at **www.eduplace.com/kids/hmss/**

In Your Classroom

Look for these Social Studies Independent Books in your classroom.

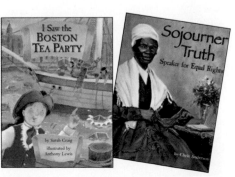

At the Library

You may find these books at your school or public library.

Life in a Colonial Town
by Sally Senzell Isaacs

Thomas Edison
by Lola Schaefer

UNIT 6

America's Government

"My country 'tis of thee,
Sweet land of liberty,
Of thee I sing."

Samuel Francis Smith,
from the song "America," 1831

The Big Idea

What does government mean to you and your family?

Vocabulary Preview

Technology

e • **glossary**
e • **word games**
www.eduplace.com/kids/hmss/

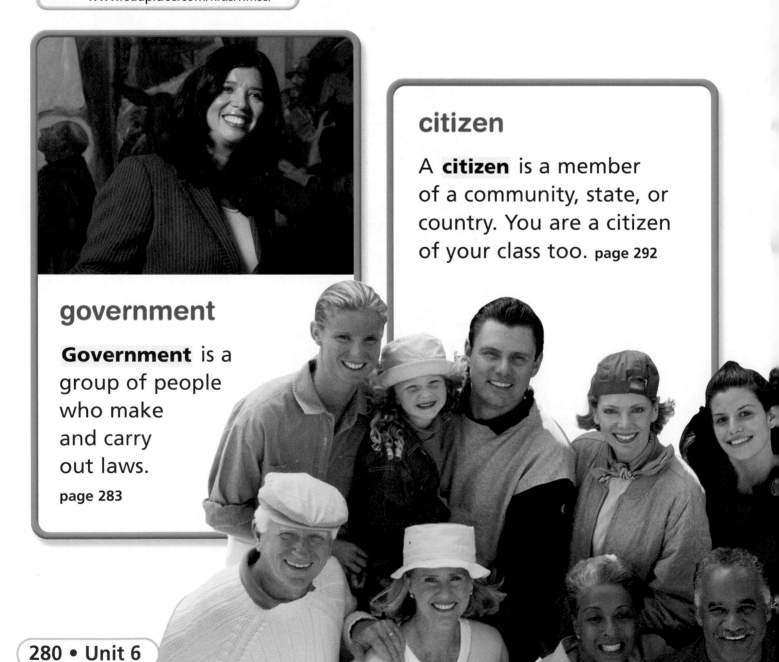

citizen

A **citizen** is a member of a community, state, or country. You are a citizen of your class too. page 292

government

Government is a group of people who make and carry out laws.

page 283

Reading Strategy

Use the **summarize** reading strategy in Lessons 1, 2, and 3 and the **question** strategy in Lessons 4, 5, and 6.

election

An **election** is a time when people vote. You can hold a class election to make a choice. page 308

Constitution

The **Constitution** is a plan for making rules for the United States government. page 316

Government and People

▶ **Vocabulary**

government
capital
tax

◎ **Reading Skill**
Draw Conclusions

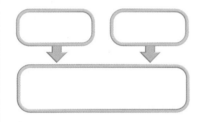

STANDARDS
Core: HSS 2.3
Extend support: HSS 2.3

Build on What You Know

Who are the people who help run your school? What are some ways they work together?

Communities are like schools. A community needs a group of people working together to help it run well.

A school principal raises the flag with the help of students.

Most communities have a city or town hall building where people work to run local government.

Local Government

A **government** is a group of people who work together to run a community, state, or country. The government of a community is called a local government. People in your local government decide how to use money for schools, police, and other community needs. They try to solve community problems too.

main idea (★)

Review What do people in government do?

Three Governments

Your state also has a government. Each state has a **capital,** which is a city where the people in government work. The United States has a government, too. That is the national government. It is in Washington, D.C., the nation's capital. Everyone has three governments: local, state, and national.

Look at Robin, for example.

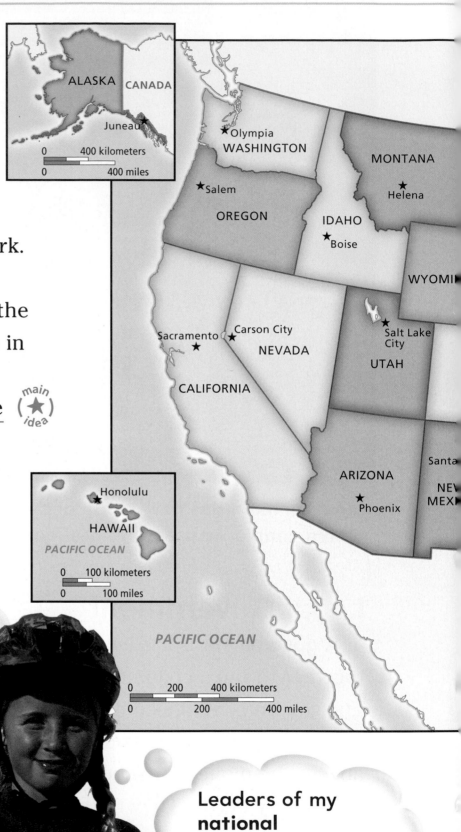

main idea (★)

I live in Duluth, Minnesota. Leaders of my **local** government meet in Duluth.

Leaders of my **state** government meet in St. Paul, the capital of Minnesota.

Leaders of my **national** government meet in Washington, D.C.

The United States of America

Skill **Reading Maps** Find Duluth, Minnesota. Is Duluth north, or south, of the state capital of Minnesota?

Government Services

Remember the services you read about in Unit 4. Fixing cars and cutting hair are services. Governments have many services for people too. Local, state, and national governments each help with different services. Here are some examples.

(main ★ idea)

Services

Local Government

schools
firefighters
libraries
police

State Government

state colleges
state parks
state roads

National Government

National Park Service
U.S. Post Office
Coast Guard

Taxes

How do governments pay for services? Governments collect money called **taxes.** Workers pay income taxes from the money they earn. Businesses also pay income taxes. In most states, people pay sales taxes when they buy goods such as bikes or baseballs. Governments use money from taxes to pay for services such as parks, police, and roads.

Review Why do governments need taxes?

	35.00
Baseball Bat	8.00
Baseball	40.00
Baseball glove	
	83.00
SUBTOTAL	3.32
Georgia Tax 4.00%	$86.32
TOTAL	
	90.00
Cash	3.68
Cash Change	

Lesson Review

❶ **Vocabulary** Write a sentence that explains what **taxes** are.

❷ **Main Idea** What are the three governments that people have?

Activity Write a summary for the section titled "Three Governments."

1. HSS 2.3 2. HSS 2.3 **Activity** HSS 2.3

Fire Fighters

From **The Fire Station** by Stuart A. Kallen

When a fire alarm rings, fire fighters race into action. Fire fighters are men and women who risk their lives every day. Their most important job is to put out fires that threaten lives and property. They must learn how to do this at fire fighters' school.

Fire fighters drive long red fire trucks to help pump the water onto fires. Huge hoses shoot water onto fires. Fire fighters use ladders to climb into the windows of burning buildings. They use axes to break through burning doors and walls.

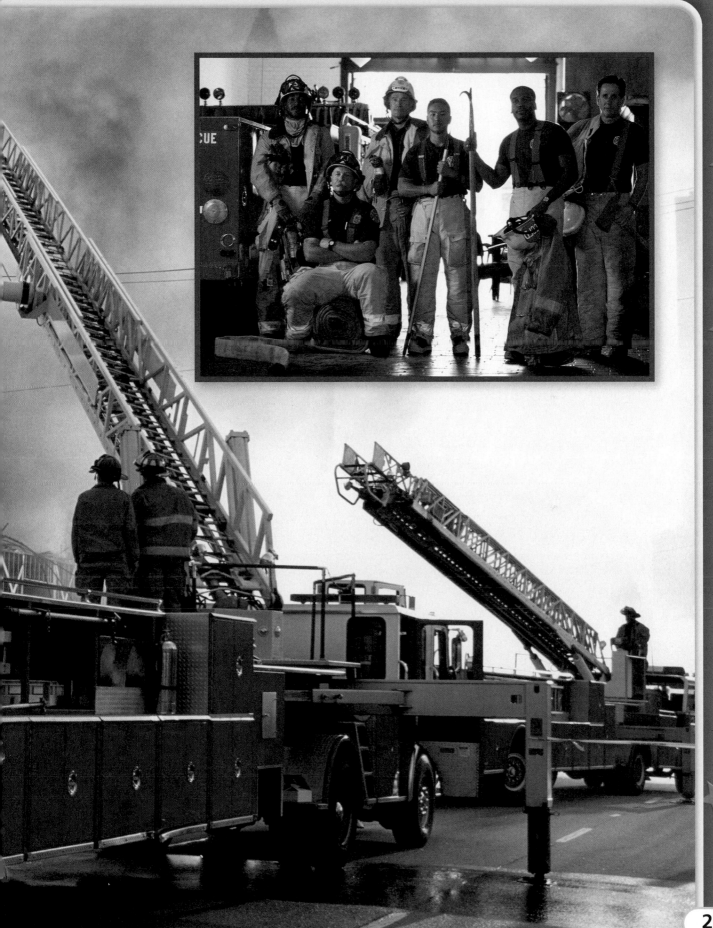

Fighting fires is hard, dangerous work. Sometimes fire fighters lose their lives in fires. Almost every city and town has a monument to fire fighters. Some are honored with medals and decorations.

Fire fighters don't just rescue people. They rescue dogs, cats and other pets.

You can be sure that if there is an emergency a firefighter will be there as soon as possible.

A fire fighter uses an extension ladder to get water to fires in skyscrapers.

A fire fighters' memorial

Activities

1. **Talk About It** Draw a fire fighter at work. Tell about your drawing.

2. **Write About It** Write about how a fire fighter shows courage.

Citizens Make a Difference

Vocabulary

citizen
right
responsibility

Reading Skill
Classify

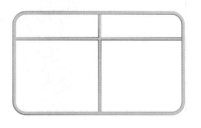

STANDARDS

Core: HSS 2.3, 2.5
Extend support: HSS 2.3.2

Build on What You Know

Think of ways students have made your school a good place to learn. You will read about how you are a citizen in your school, community, and nation.

You Are a Citizen

A **citizen** is a person who belongs to a place. You are a citizen of the community where you live and the nation where you were born. You can also become a citizen of the United States even if you were not born here.

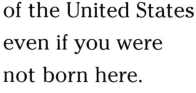

Citizens Have Rights

As a citizen, you have rights that the government protects. A **right** is something you may do. As a citizen of the United States, you have a right to speak freely and to practice your religion. In the past, American Indians, African Americans, and women were not allowed to vote. They had to speak out for their rights to vote and to be treated fairly.

Review What rights do you have as a citizen?

RIGHTS

Speak Freely

Worship

Be Equal

Citizens Have Responsibilities

Along with rights, citizens have responsibilities. _{main} (★) _{idea}
A **responsibility** is something that you should do. A responsibility may be following rules or doing a chore. It may be treating others fairly. Name some responsibilities you have. What would happen if you did not do them?

Skill **Reading Visuals** What are the citizens doing for their community?

Being a Good Citizen

Good citizens care about people's rights. They try to make things fair and safe for everyone. Good citizens work together to solve problems. Children can be good citizens by solving problems together in their school or community. Look at the four steps.

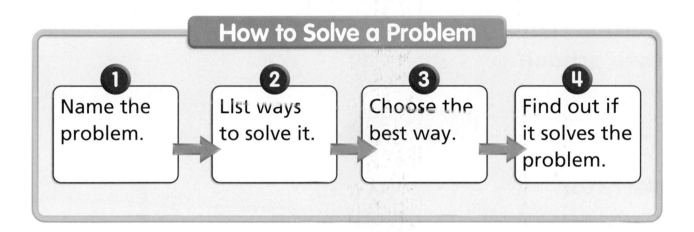

How to Solve a Problem

1 Name the problem.

2 List ways to solve it.

3 Choose the best way.

4 Find out if it solves the problem.

Review How can you be a good citizen?

Lesson Review

1 **Vocabulary** Name two **rights** of **citizens** in the United States.

2 **Main Idea** Copy this sentence. Fill in the blanks. Citizens of the United States have _____ and _____.

Activity Draw a poster that shows how to be a good citizen. Write sentences to explain your ideas.

1. HSS 2.3 **2.** HSS 2.3 **Activity** HSS 2.3

Solving Problems

Read about some students who take **responsibility** to try to solve a problem at their school.

Cast

Narrator

Lisa: student

Greg: student

Mimi: student

Don: student

Mr. Vacca: teacher

Ms. Leroy: principal

Scene 1

Narrator: We are in Mr. Vacca's classroom. It's a Friday in May. Our class is almost ready to go home. Then the principal, Ms. Leroy, speaks on the intercom.

Ms. Leroy: Next week the builders will start the new addition to our school. They will have to take out all the bike racks. After that, no one can ride a bike to school.

Lisa: So we can't ride our bikes to school all spring!

Mr. Vacca: Everyone listen, please!

Ms. Leroy: Please make sure to take my letter home to your families. It tells why students cannot ride bikes to school.

Mr. Vacca: Now everyone may go, quietly! Have a good weekend.

Don: How can we have a good weekend with bad news like that?

Mimi: Maybe it will be good if we can solve the bike problem!

Lisa: Let's meet at the bike racks to talk about it.

Scene 2

Narrator: Lisa, Greg, Mimi, and Don meet at the bike racks.

Lisa: First we have to name the problem.

Greg: The problem is we want to ride our bikes to school, but now we can't.

Lisa: Next we should name the reasons why we can't ride our bikes.

Greg: Because they're building where the bike racks are.

Mimi: Then let's tell them not to build!

Don: But we want them to build. They are building a theater and a new gym.

Mimi: What if we hid Ms. Leroy's letter from our families and rode our bikes anyway?

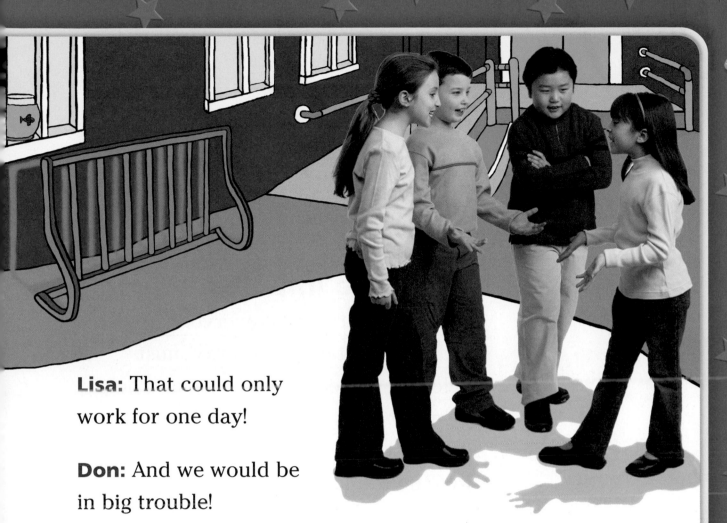

Lisa: That could only work for one day!

Don: And we would be in big trouble!

Greg: Here's another idea. Maybe they can move the bike racks to the other side of the school.

Lisa: That should work! Let's go talk to Ms. Leroy.

Don: I'll bet she'll listen. She likes kids to show responsibility. Maybe she can help us think of another way to solve the problem if our idea doesn't work.

Activities

1. **Think About It** Do you like the way the students tried to solve the problem? Why?

2. **Write About It** Write or tell what Ms. Leroy might say when the students talk to her.

299

Laws

Build on What You Know

What are some rules in your school or classroom? Learn how they are like rules in a community, state, or country.

Vocabulary

law

judge

Reading Skill

Main Idea and Details

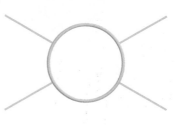

Laws Are Important

A **law** is a rule that everyone in a community, state, or country must follow. Laws keep people safe and help them get along with one another. What do you think would happen if there were no traffic laws?

Review Why are laws important?

STANDARDS

Core: HSS 2.3.1, 2.5
Extend support: HSS 2.3.1, 2.5

The signs on this page tell people about laws.

Police stop drivers who speed.

Police Help with Laws

Local, state, and national governments have laws. Police help with government laws. They tell people how to obey (oh BAY) laws. They stop people who break laws. Look at the picture on this page. What do you think is happening? Think of another way that police help with laws.

main
(★)
idea

In Court Judges work in courts where people come when they have problems with laws. Here two lawyers talk to a judge.

Judges Help with Laws

A **judge** is someone who helps when people don't agree about laws. Governments have many, many laws. Judges know the laws well. They help decide if someone has broken a law. Judges say what people must do to make up for breaking laws.

main idea (★)

Citizens Help with Laws

Citizens protect each other when they know and follow laws. When people obey a traffic law, they help keep others safe. When you follow laws in a park, you help others enjoy the park. Citizens help by choosing good people to make laws. Also citizens can work together to make better laws.

main idea (★)

States have laws about driving. In many states, you must be sixteen before you can get a permit to learn to drive.

Review What can citizens do to help with laws?

Lesson Review

1 Vocabulary Tell two things that **judges** do.

2 Main Idea What would happen if drivers did not pay attention to traffic lights?

✏️ **Activity** Name a law that you think is important. Write or tell why you think it is important.

1. HSS 2.3.1 2. HSS 2.3.1 **Activity** HSS 2.3.1

Rosa Parks

Rosa Parks in 1999

Not everyone is brave enough to risk jail for what they believe is right. In 1955, Rosa Parks showed courage when she stood up for her beliefs.

At that time Rosa Parks was living in Montgomery, Alabama. The state's **laws** and rules did not give African American people the same rights as white people. This seemed very wrong to Rosa Parks. She began to work with others who wanted fair laws and rights for everyone.

Rosa Parks helped change a law that was unfair to African American people on buses.

Taking Action

On December 1, 1955, Rosa Parks acted against an unfair law. The law made African Americans give up their bus seats to white people.

Rosa Parks stayed firmly in her seat when the bus driver tried to make her give it up. For this she had to go to jail. Her action led many others to work together to change the unfair law.

Activities

1. **Talk About It** How did Rosa Parks show courage?

2. **Build It** Make a mobile that shows pictures of citizens who did something brave.

Read a Pictograph

▶ **Vocabulary**

pictograph

A school started a project to recycle cans. The children used a pictograph to keep track of the cans they collected.

Learn the Skill

A **pictograph** is a way to compare things. A pictograph uses pictures to show numbers of things.

Step 1 Look at the title. It tells what the pictograph is about.

Step 2 Look at the key. It shows what each picture of a can stands for.

Step 3 Count the cans for Class A. There are seven cans. So Class A collected seven 10s, or seventy, cans.

NET WT. 16O

Look at the graph below. Then follow the directions.

1 What is the title of this pictograph?

2 How many cans did Class C collect?

3 How many cans did Class E collect?

4 How many cans did Classes B and D collect together?

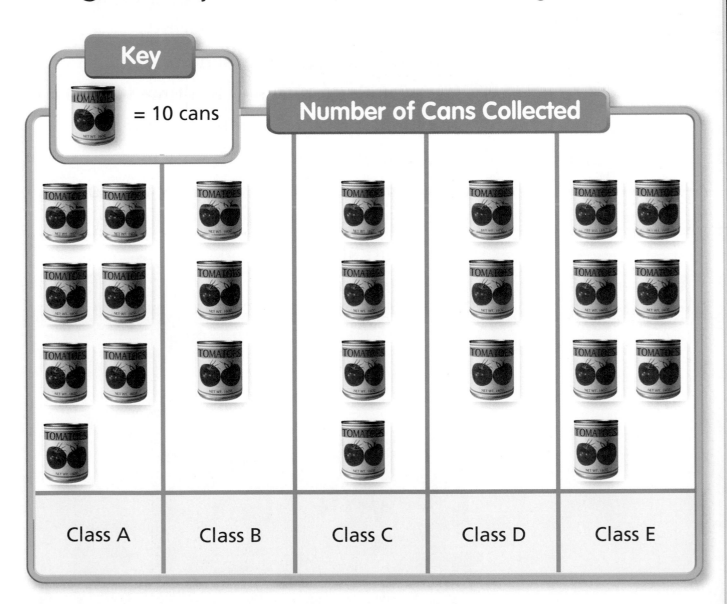

Key

= 10 cans

Number of Cans Collected

Class A   Class B   Class C   Class D   Class E

▶ **Vocabulary**

vote
election
ballot

🎯 **Reading Skill**

Sequence

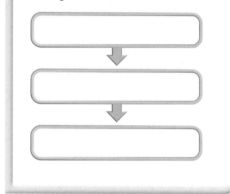

STANDARDS
Core: HSS 2.3, 2.3.1
Extend support: HSS 2.3

Leaders

Build on What You Know

Sports teams and school bands have leaders. What are some other kinds of leaders? Governments have leaders too.

Choosing Leaders

Did you ever choose a leader for a team? When you show or write a choice, you **vote.** Your school might have an **election,** which is a time when people vote. When you turn eighteen, you will have the right to vote in government elections. You may vote for many different leaders in one election. The chart shows three examples.

main idea

Government Leaders

Local Government
Citizens may vote for mayor of their city or town.

State Government
Citizens may vote for governor of the state where they live.

National Government
Citizens may vote for President of the United States.

main idea

Government leaders have important jobs. Some make laws. Others make sure the laws work well. In elections, citizens get to choose leaders who they think can do these jobs the best.

Review Why should citizens vote in government elections?

Before You Vote

What can citizens do to choose the best leaders?
They can read newspapers and watch television.
They can ask questions of leaders. They can ask
themselves questions.

Will you add more bus stops?

What can you do to fix our playgrounds?

My Questions

★ Is this person honest and smart?

★ Will this person work hard for all citizens?

★ Can this person run the government best?

Leaders and Citizens

A **ballot** is a form on which people mark their choices. In elections, citizens vote on ballots.

Leaders who win elections need to keep listening to citizens. Citizens need to keep telling leaders what they want for their community, state, and country. Citizens and leaders together help governments work well. (★ main idea)

People who run for election explain how they will work for citizens.

Review Why should leaders talk with citizens?

Lesson Review

❶ **Vocabulary** Use the words **vote** and **election** to tell some things you know about leaders.

❷ **Main Idea** Tell something that government leaders do.

▶ **Activity** Write or tell two things a voter can do before an election.

Voting with Ballots

The eagle is a symbol for our national government. You can choose an animal to be a symbol for your class. Think of animals that stand for something you feel proud about, such as being kind or smart.

Choose between the two animals you see on the box, or decide on two different animals to choose from. Have an **election** in your classroom. Use a ballot to mark your choice. Then count the votes to know the winning symbol for your class.

1   Look at the two animals. Think about their special features. Decide which is the best symbol for your class. Make speeches and signs.

2   Mark your ballot with your choice. Do not write your name on your ballot! It's a secret vote. Add your ballot to a big box.

3   Help count the votes for each animal. Write down the totals. Check your counts and totals. Which symbol won? Plan together how to show your new class symbol.

Resolve a Conflict

▶ **Vocabulary**

conflict

People in classrooms and communities don't always agree. When people disagree, it is called a **conflict.** Together, people can resolve conflicts.

Learn the Skill

Follow the steps to help resolve a conflict.

Step 1 Look at the picture. Describe the conflict. Two children want to use the computer at the same time.

Step 2 Think about what each child wants to do.

Write	Play Games

Step 3 Think of ways to resolve the conflict.

- Take turns.
- Writer uses pencil.
- Game player plays board game.

Step 4 Ask yourself about each idea: Can both children do some of what they want? Choose the best way to resolve the conflict.

Practice the Skill

STANDARDS HSS 2.3.2

Work with a small group. Look at the picture below. Then follow the directions.

1 Tell in your own words what the conflict is. What does each group want?

2 List some ways to resolve the conflict.

3 Choose the best solution. Tell why your solution is the best one.

National Government

Vocabulary

Constitution
democracy
liberty
justice

Reading Skill

Classify

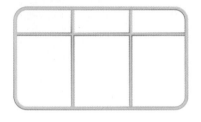

STANDARDS

Core: HSS 2.3
Extend support: HSS 2.3

Build on What You Know

When you start a class project, you may write a plan for how it will work. In a way, that is like the plan that early leaders wrote for our nation's government.

A Plan for Government

In Unit 5 you read about the Revolutionary War. When that war ended, American leaders did not want a king to rule the new nation. The leaders met and wrote a new plan for the government. That plan is called the **Constitution.**

main idea

Review What is the Constitution?

Important Words

The writers of the Constitution planned a **democracy,** which is government by the people. They used words that they believed were important in a democracy. One word was **liberty,** which means "freedom." Another was **justice,** which means "fairness." Why are they still important words today?

Government in Three Parts

The Constitution is more than 200 years old. It is still the plan for our government today. <u>The Constitution describes a government in three parts, or branches.</u> Each branch has its own building in Washington, D.C. On these pages you can read about the people who work in those buildings.

main ★ idea

Review How many branches does the government have?

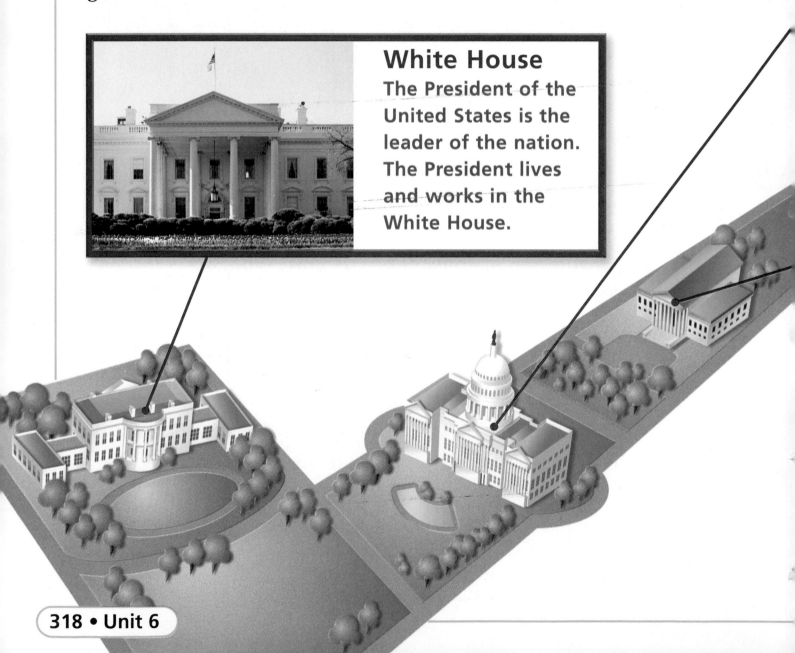

White House

The President of the United States is the leader of the nation. The President lives and works in the White House.

Capitol

The members of Congress make laws. Men and women in Congress come from all fifty states. They work in the Capitol Building.

Supreme Court

The Supreme Court has nine judges who look carefully at laws. They decide if the laws are fair and protect citizens' rights. They meet in the Supreme Court Building.

Lesson Review

① **Vocabulary** When do you say, "with **liberty** and **justice** for all"? Tell what it means.

② **Main Idea** What are the three branches of the national government?

Activity Make a chart that shows who works in the three branches of government.

1. HSS 2.3 2. HSS 2.3, HSS 2.3

Democracy

Democracy is government that comes from the people. In a democracy, people make choices about their leaders and their laws. They may do this by voting in an election.

In the United States, citizens may vote for a leader of their community or state. They may also vote for a few people from their state to go to Washington, D.C. Those people are members of Congress. In Congress, they vote to make laws for all citizens in the country. Look at examples of democracy in the United States.

School

Students vote on where to have their class picnic.

Community

This city council votes on how much money to spend on city services.

Democracy in Action

Nation

People vote for a new President of the United States.

State

People hear a speech before they vote for governor.

Activities

1. **Talk About It** Tell how democracy is part of what happens in your class or school.

2. **Write About It** Write about why voting is important in a democracy.

Our Nation and the World

Vocabulary

aid

Reading Skill

Problem and Solution

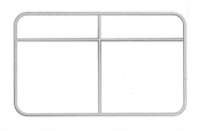

STANDARDS

Core: HSS 2.3.2
Extend support: Analysis Skill HI 2

Build on What You Know

Have you ever worked with a friend to solve a problem? Sometimes nations work together to try to solve problems.

Nations Help Each Other

The United States is one of more than two hundred nations in the world. Nations work out ways to help each other. If storms destroy crops in one nation, other nations may send aid. **Aid** is help. It can be money, goods, or services. What goods or services might people need after a big storm?

U.S. troops give bags of food to people in Honduras after a hurricane.

United States President Jimmy Carter sits between President Anwar el-Sadat of Egypt (left) and Prime Minister Menachem Begin of Israel after the signing of a peace treaty between Israel and Egypt.

Leaders Work Together

(★) main idea

Every nation has a government. <u>Government leaders from different nations work together.</u> They talk about how to make the earth cleaner and safer. Leaders have meetings about trade, health, and peace. Government leaders travel to visit each other. They stay in touch by phone, mail, and the Internet.

Review Why do leaders from different countries work together?

Meetings Around the World

Here are a few places where world leaders have met to discuss problems.

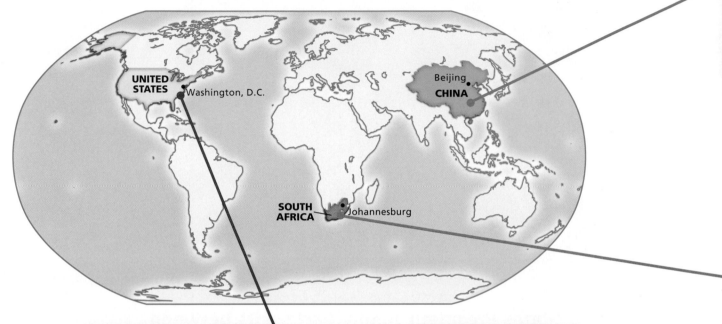

United States

President George W. Bush met in Washington, D.C. with President Vladimir Putin from Russia.

China

Jiang Zemin, the president of China (left) met with Prime Minister Tony Blair of Great Britain in Beijing.

South Africa

Palestinian leader Yasir Arafat met with President Nelson Mandela of South Africa in Johannesburg.

Review Why are meetings with leaders from different countries important?

Lesson Review

❶ **Vocabulary** Give an example of government **aid.**

❷ **Main Idea** What are two ways that government leaders from different countries stay in touch?

Activity Choose a leader whose country is not shown on the map on page 324. Find his or her country on a world map.

Flags of Different Nations

Did you know that there are more than 200 nations in the world? Every one of them has a different flag.

I live in **Mexico**. The eagle holding a snake is important in a legend of our country. Red, white, and green stand for our independence.

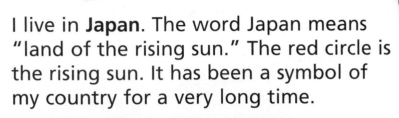

I live in **Japan**. The word Japan means "land of the rising sun." The red circle is the rising sun. It has been a symbol of my country for a very long time.

I live in **Ghana** in Africa. The black star on our flag is a symbol of freedom. The stripes have colors that are important in the flags of many African nations.

Activities

1. **Talk About It** What is one way that the three flags are alike?

2. **Write About It** Write something you learned about one of the three flags.

327

Unit 6

Big Ideas

The Big Idea

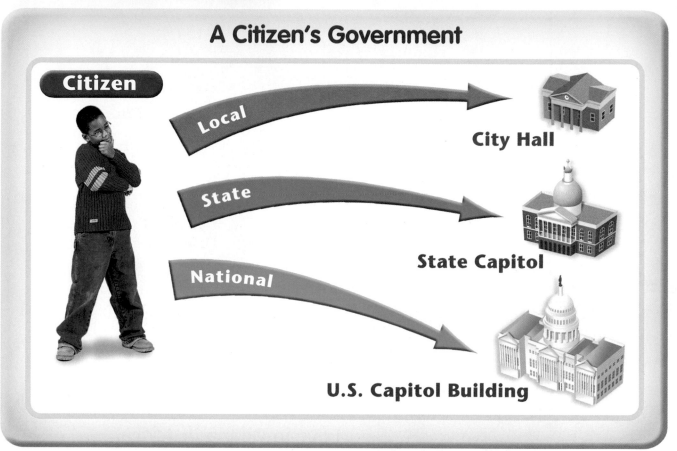

A Citizen's Government

Citizen

Local → **City Hall**

State → **State Capitol**

National → **U.S. Capitol Building**

Fill in three missing words that help describe the chart.

Each citizen has **1.** _____ , **2.** _____ , and **3.** _____ governments. (page 284)

STANDARDS **1.** HSS 2.3 **2.** HSS 2.3 **3.** HSS 2.3

Facts and Main Ideas

4. Why do governments collect taxes? (page 287)

5. What is one responsibility that citizens have? (page 294)

6. What are two things citizens can do to choose good leaders? (page 310)

7. What is the Constitution? (page 316)

4. HSS 2.3 **5.** HSS 2.5 **6.** HSS 2.5 **7.** HSS 2.3

Write the letter of the correct answer.

8. The money that people pay to a government

9. A person who belongs to a place

10. A freedom that government must protect

11. A time when people vote

8. HSS 2.4 9. HSS 2.3 10. HSS 2.3 11. HSS 2.3 12. HSS 2.3

A. **right** (page 293)

B. **election** (page 308)

C. **taxes** (page 287)

D. **citizen** (page 292)

E. **judge** (page 302)

✓ Test Practice

12. What does the word **government** mean?

   A. A person who belongs to a place, such as a state

   B. A group of people who make and carry out laws

   C. A leader of a community, state, or country

   D. Something that people should do for others

Critical Thinking

Compare and Contrast

13. What are some ways that your local government is like your national government?

14. What are some ways that your local government is different from your national government?

13. HSS 2.3 14. HSS 2.3.1

Review

Read a Pictograph

Mrs. Tan's class is choosing a place for a field trip. The pictograph shows the class's votes.

Votes for Our Field Trip	
Aquarium	✔✔✔✔✔✔
Fire Station	✔✔✔
Bakery	✔✔✔✔
Dairy Farm	✔✔✔✔✔✔

15. Which choice has the most votes?

16. Which has the fewest?

17. How many children voted?

15. HSS 2.3 16. HSS 2.3 17. HSS 2.3

Resolve a Conflict

Jack, Lena, Darryl, and Kay all want another slice of pizza. There are only 2 slices of pizza left.

18. Choose the best way to resolve the conflict.

18. HSS 2.4.3

A   B   C

Unit Activity

Make Up a Riddle

Think of a person, place, or thing you learned about in this unit. You might choose a government leader or service worker. Keep your choice secret.

❶ Fold a sheet of paper in half and write two riddle clues on the outside. Write your secret answer inside.

❷ Show your clues to others. Can they guess?

MY
Clues
1. a plan
2. rights

Current Events

Current Events Project

Find out what your local government is doing. Make a **Government in the News Big Book**.

Government
in the News

Technology

Read articles about current events at **www.eduplace.com/kids/hmss/**

In Your Classroom

Look for these Social Studies Independent Books in your classroom.

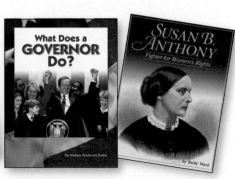

At the Library

You may find these books at your school or public library.

We the Kids
by David Catrow

City Green
by DyAnne DiSalvo-Ryan

Veterans Day

Veterans Day honors people who were in the army and other armed forces. Soldiers, sailors, and pilots who served the United States are veterans.

Many veterans march in Veterans Day parades. People thank our veterans for helping our country when it is at war and at peace.

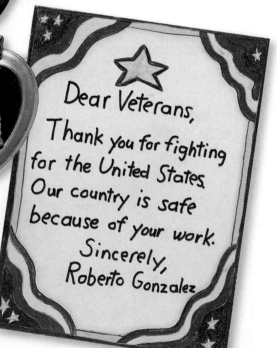

A Purple Heart medal

Dear Veterans,
Thank you for fighting for the United States. Our country is safe because of your work.
Sincerely,
Roberto Gonzalez

Activity

Thank You Letter

1. Write a thank you letter to a veteran.

2. You may display your letter or mail it to a group of veterans.

Thanksgiving

On Thanksgiving Day people give thanks for what they have. This is a tradition that comes from harvest festivals long ago. The Pilgrims shared their first harvest with the Wampanoag.

In 1863, President Abraham Lincoln thought the United States should have a day of thanks. He started the national holiday we celebrate today.

American families of many backgrounds celebrate Thanksgiving Day. People may eat foods from their own culture. Many people also eat turkey and cranberry sauce. Many families talk about why they feel thankful. Some go to church.

Activity

Thanksgiving Stick Puppets

1. Make stick puppets of the Pilgrims and the Wampanoag.

2. What do you think the Pilgrims and the Wampanoag felt thankful for? Use the puppets to act out your ideas.

STANDARDS HSS 2.5, Analysis Skill HI 1

Martin Luther King, Jr. Day

Dr. Martin Luther King, Jr., worked to make laws that would be fair to all people. Each year, Americans honor his work.

Like many people, Dr. King knew that some laws were not fair to African Americans. He gave speeches and marched to show the need to change the unfair laws. He shared his dream of good lives for all. He received the Nobel Peace Prize for his work.

Activity

Dream Doves

1. Think of a dream that you believe is good for everyone.

2. Write your dream on the shape of a dove.

Presidents' Day

On Presidents' Day, people honor two important Presidents of the United States.

George Washington helped make the United States a free country. He led the army for the new country in the American Revolution. He was the first President of the United States.

Abraham Lincoln was another great President. He helped to make all people in the United States equal and free. Lincoln helped keep the states together in one country.

Activity

"If I Am President" Poster

1. Think about what you would do if you were the President of the United States.

2. Make a poster to show your ideas.

Jenny for President !!!
I will:
plant trees
clean up trash
give children books

Memorial Day

Vietnam Veterans Memorial

On Memorial Day, citizens of the United States remember the people who fought and died in wars.

A memorial is something that helps people remember a person, a group, or an event from the past. A memorial can be a statue, a sign, or a building. On Memorial Day, people gather at memorials and cemeteries.

People put flowers and flags on memorials and graves. Towns and cities have parades or speeches. Citizens honor the people who fought for the United States.

Activity

Make a Memorial Circle

1. Think of a person or an event you want to remember.

2. Write the words on a circle of colored paper. You may add a picture.

In memory of my grandpa Ted Barrios

In memory of people who fought in all wars

Flag Day

The United States flag stands for our country. On Flag Day, many communities have parades and sing the national anthem.

Our country's first flag had only 13 stripes and 13 stars. They stood for the 13 colonies that formed our country. Later the colonies became states.

Now there are 50 states in the United States. The United States flag has 50 stars that stand for our 50 states. It still has 13 stripes.

Activity

State Stars

1. Cut out the shape of a white star.

2. Write the name of a state in red. Write the capital of the state in blue.

337

STANDARDS Analysis Skill HI 1

Independence Day

On the Fourth of July, we celebrate our country's birthday.

The United States was started on July 4, 1776. On that day, our leaders signed an important paper. It said that our land and our people were now free from Great Britain.

Independence is another word for **freedom**. Every Fourth of July, we celebrate our country's freedom. Towns and cities have parades and picnics. Many communities have fireworks at night.

Activity

Freedom Poem

1. Think of some things that United States citizens are free to do.

2. Write a poem about your freedoms. You may start with the words "I am free. . . ."

I am free to read books and talk to people.

I am free to think and learn.

I am free to be me!

References

Citizenship Handbook

Our Flag R2

Songs of Our Nation R4

Character Traits R8

Resources

Geographic Terms R10

Atlas R12

Picture Glossary R20

Index R36

Primary Source References R46

Acknowledgments R49

Our Flag

Pledge of Allegiance

I **pledge allegiance** to the flag
of the United States of America
and to the **Republic** for which it stands,
one Nation under God, **indivisible,**
with **liberty** and **justice** for all.

**What does the Pledge of Allegiance mean?
Use the vocabulary to explain.**

pledge: promise
allegiance: loyalty
republic: nation
indivisible: cannot be divided
liberty: freedom
justice: fairness

Rules about the Flag

Look at some rules about our national flag. They come from a law called the United States Flag Code.

-  The flag should have thirteen stripes, red and white. It should have white stars on a blue background. It should have a star for each state.

- To salute the flag, stand straight and face the flag. Put your right hand on your heart.

- Say the pledge while you salute.

- 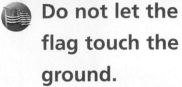 Do not let the flag touch the ground.

- Fly the United States flag above any state flag.

- At night, take down the flag or light it up.

Songs of Our Nation

On page 143, you can read the words to "The Star-Spangled Banner," our national anthem. Many other songs also show our pride in our country. How did they come to be?

In 1893, a teacher from the East named Katharine Lee Bates took a trip to the West. The beauty of mountains, plains, and open skies inspired her to write a poem. Bates's poem became the words for the song "America the Beautiful."

"America the Beautiful"

by Katharine Lee Bates

O beautiful for spacious skies,
   For amber waves of grain,
For purple mountain majesties
   Above the fruited plain.
America! America!
   God shed His grace on thee
And crown thy good with brotherhood
   From sea to shining sea.

Vocabulary

spacious: spread over a large area

amber: golden brown

majesties: powers

fruited: successfully planted

shed: give out

grace: blessing

thee: you

brotherhood: friendship

What does the song mean to you?
The words above help explain the song.

Samuel F. Smith heard the British national anthem in 1832 and liked the music. He wrote words so that Americans could sing it. "America," or "My Country, 'Tis of Thee," quickly became a favorite of many people in the United States. People still love to sing it today.

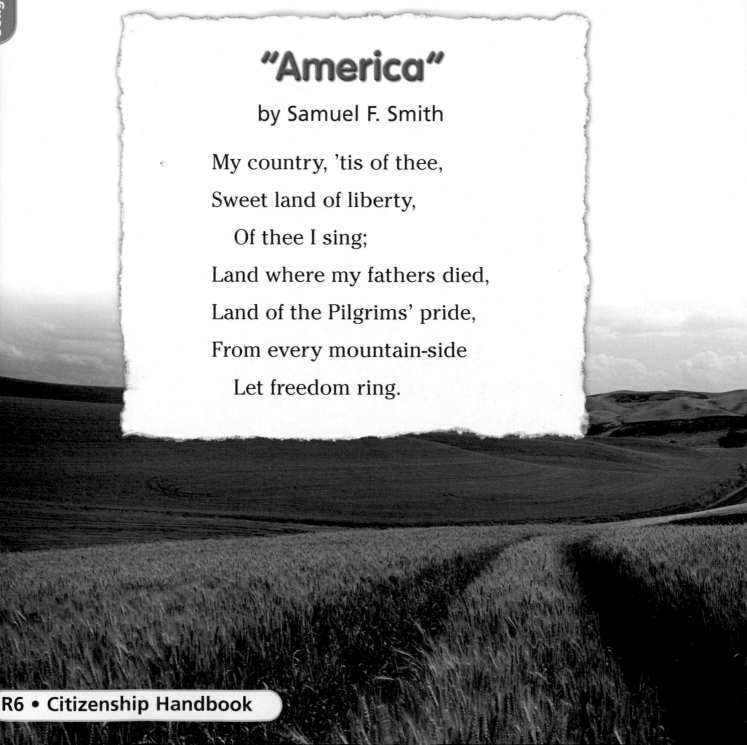

"America"

by Samuel F. Smith

My country, 'tis of thee,

Sweet land of liberty,

Of thee I sing;

Land where my fathers died,

Land of the Pilgrims' pride,

From every mountain-side

Let freedom ring.

Irving Berlin first wrote "God Bless America" for a show in 1918 but did not use it then. Twenty years later, when it seemed that war would break out at any minute, he decided to revise the song. Kate Smith, a famous singer, sang it on a radio program. People loved the song, and it has been an American favorite ever since.

"God Bless America"

by Irving Berlin

God bless America,

Land that I love,

Stand beside her and guide her

Through the night with a light from above.

From the mountains, to the prairies,

To the oceans white with foam,

God bless America,

My home sweet home.

Character Traits

A character trait is something people show by the way they act. A person who acts bravely shows courage, and courage is a character trait.

Character traits are also called "life skills." Life skills can help you do your best, and doing your best leads to reaching your goals.

Rosa Parks
Courage
Rosa Parks showed courage by acting against an unfair law.

Paul Revere
Patriotism
Paul Revere showed patriotism by riding to warn the colonists about the plans of the British army.

Courage means acting bravely. It takes courage to be honest and tell the truth.

Patriotism is being proud of your country and working for your country's goals.

Responsibility means doing all your work. You can count on people who show responsibility. They will do all the things they are asked to do.

Respect means paying attention to what other people want and believe. Treating others with respect helps everyone get along.

Fairness means acting to make things fair for everyone.

Civic virtue is good citizenship. It means doing things to help communities live and work well together.

Caring is helping others. Listening to how other people feel is also caring.

Geographic Terms

forest
a large area of land where many trees grow

hill
a raised mass of land, smaller than a mountain

▲ **desert**
a dry area where few plants grow

▲ **island**
land with water all around it

lake
a body of water with land all around it

mountains

hill

river

lake

ocean

mountain
a steep mass of land, much higher than the surrounding country

▲ **ocean**
a salty body of water covering a large area of the earth

peninsula
land that sticks out into water

plain
a broad, flat area of land

plateau
an area of flat land that is higher than the land around it

river
a large stream of water that runs into a lake, ocean, or another river

valley
low land between mountains or hills

valley

peninsula

plain

Atlas

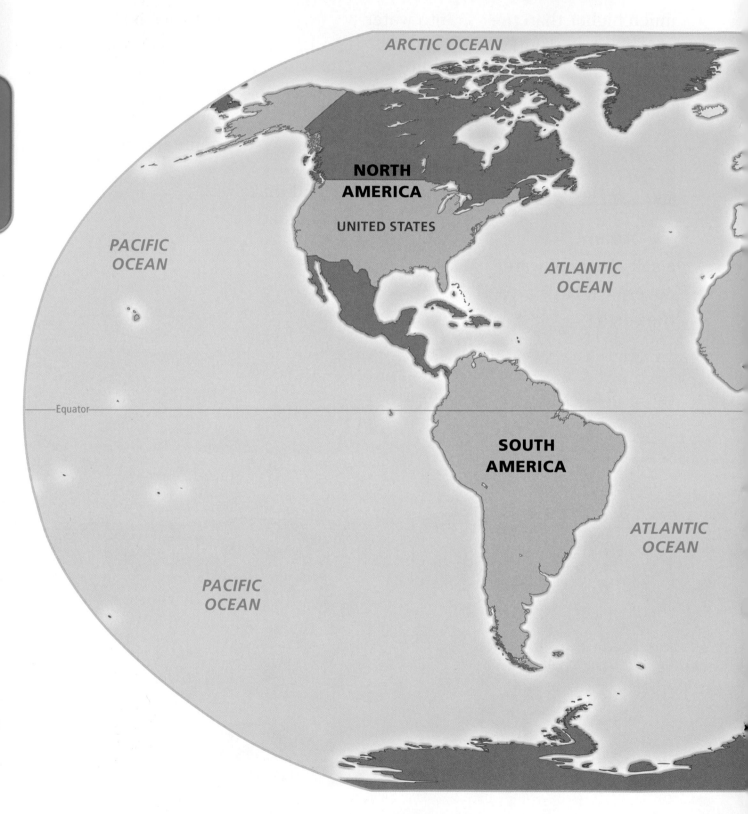

ARCTIC OCEAN

NORTH
AMERICA

UNITED STATES

PACIFIC
OCEAN

ATLANTIC
OCEAN

Equator

SOUTH
AMERICA

ATLANTIC
OCEAN

PACIFIC
OCEAN

Atlas

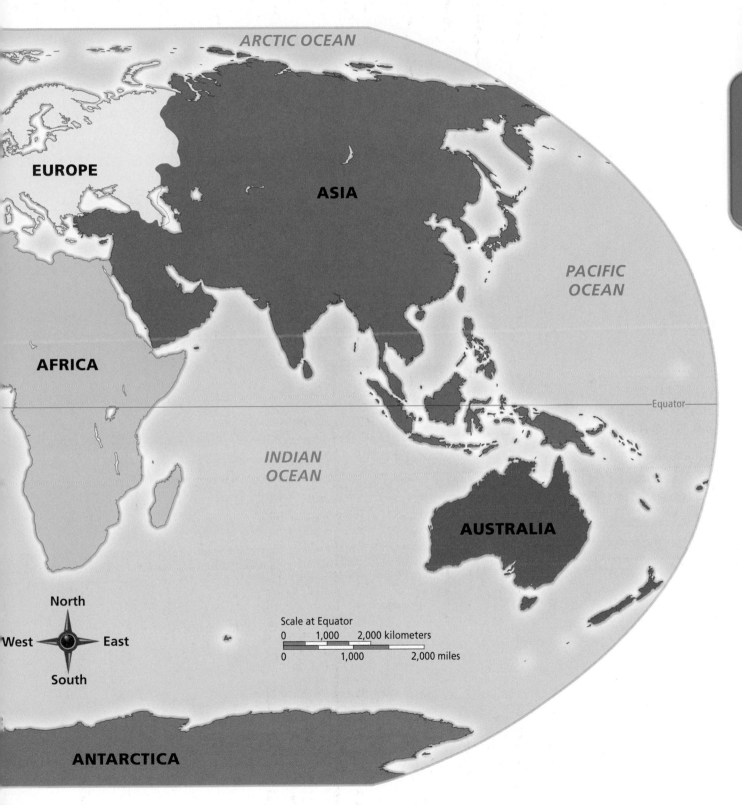

ARCTIC OCEAN

EUROPE

ASIA

PACIFIC OCEAN

AFRICA

Equator

INDIAN OCEAN

AUSTRALIA

North

West   East

South

Scale at Equator

0   1,000   2,000 kilometers

0   1,000   2,000 miles

ANTARCTICA

The World: Physical

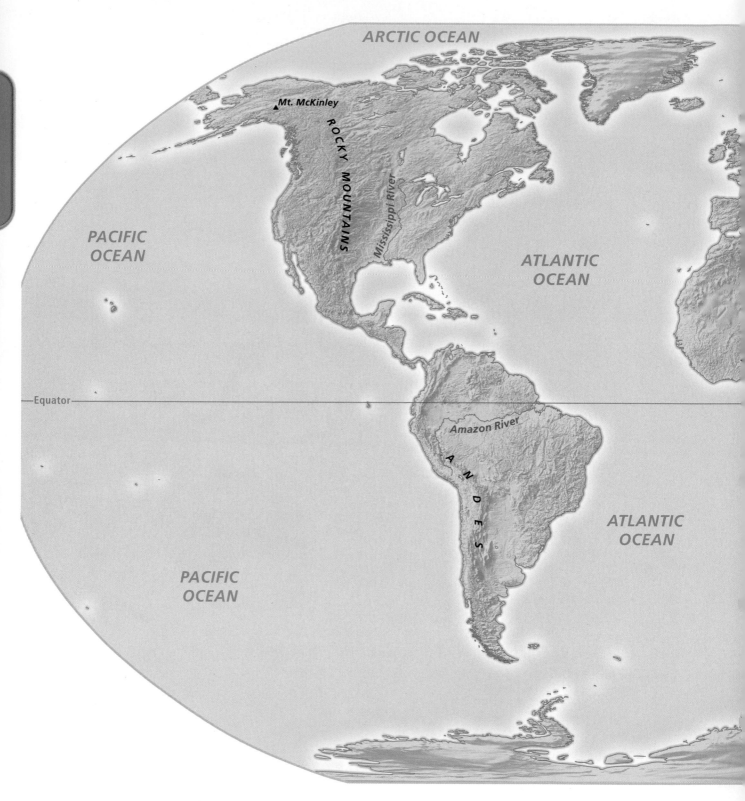

ARCTIC OCEAN

▲ Mt. McKinley

ROCKY MOUNTAINS

Mississippi River

PACIFIC OCEAN

ATLANTIC OCEAN

Equator

Amazon River

A N D E S

PACIFIC OCEAN

ATLANTIC OCEAN

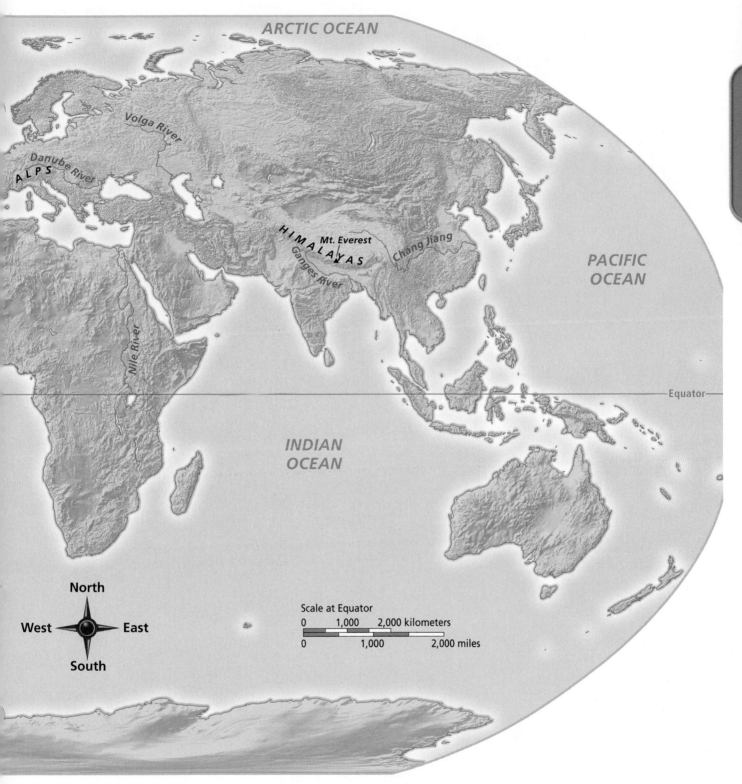

ARCTIC OCEAN

Volga River

Danube River

ALPS

Nile River

HIMALAYAS

Mt. Everest

Ganges River

Chang Jiang

PACIFIC OCEAN

Equator

INDIAN OCEAN

North

West   East

South

Scale at Equator

0   1,000   2,000 kilometers

0   1,000   2,000 miles

North America

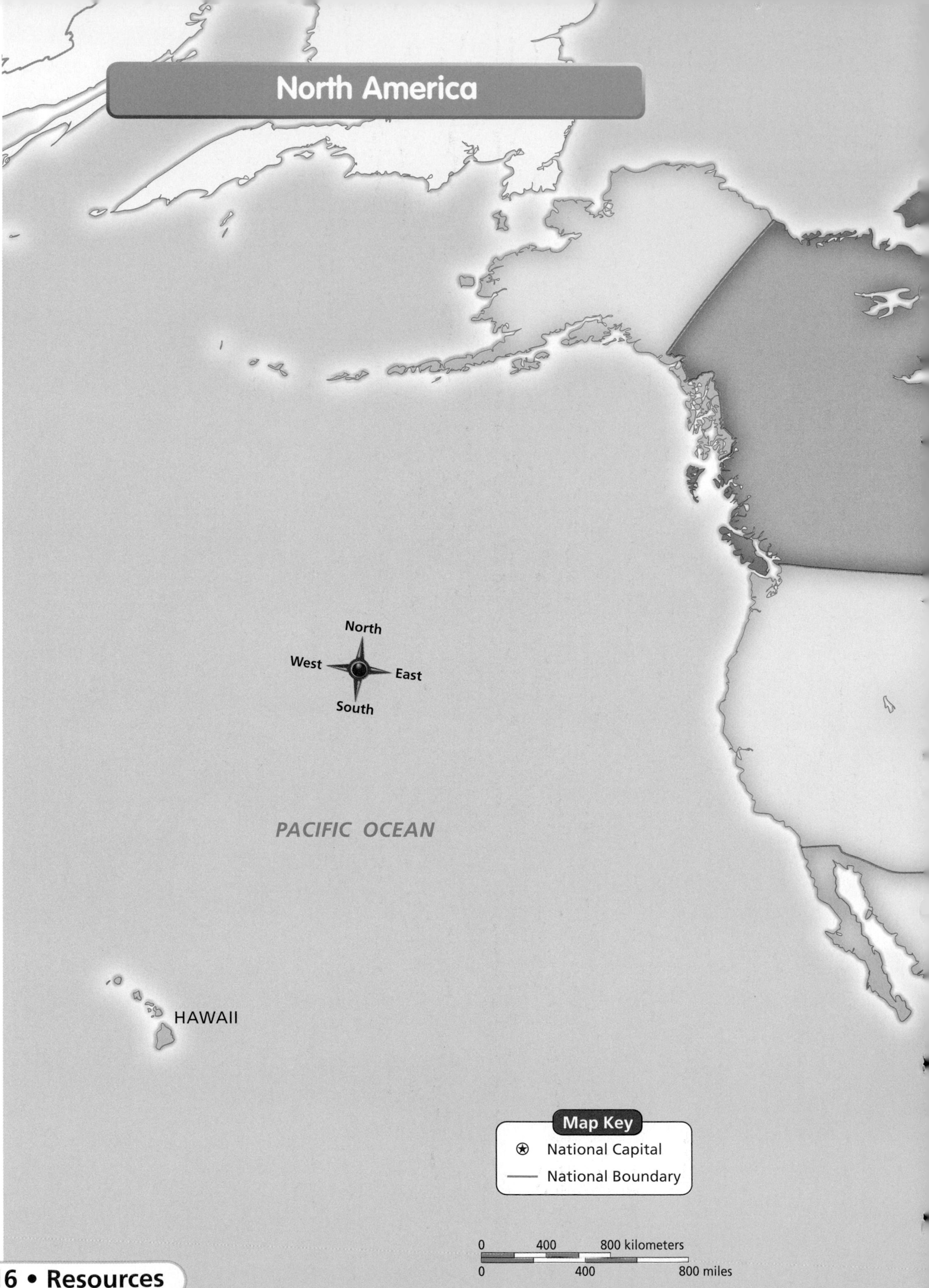

North

West — East

South

PACIFIC OCEAN

HAWAII

Map Key

⊛ National Capital

— National Boundary

0   400   800 kilometers

0   400   800 miles

GREENLAND

CANADA

Ottawa ⍟

UNITED STATES

Washington, D.C. ⍟

ATLANTIC OCEAN

Gulf of Mexico

MEXICO

Mexico City ⍟

Havana ⍟

BAHAMAS

Nassau ⍟

CUBA

JAMAICA

DOMINICAN REPUBLIC

Port-au-Prince

Santo Domingo ⍟

PUERTO RICO (U.S.)

Kingston ⍟

HAITI

Lesser Antilles

Belmopan ⍟

BELIZE

Caribbean Sea

Tegucigalpa ⍟

HONDURAS

Guatemala City ⍟

GUATEMALA

NICARAGUA

San Salvador ⍟

Managua ⍟

PANAMA

EL SALVADOR

San Jose ⍟

Panama ⍟

COSTA RICA

The United States

ALASKA

0   500 kilometers
0   500 miles

WASHINGTON

MONTANA

OREGON

IDAHO

WYOMING

North

West ⟡ East

South

NEVADA

UTAH

COLORADO

CALIFORNIA

ARIZONA

NEW
MEXICO

Map Key

⊛ National Capital

── National Boundary

── State Boundary

HAWAII

0   200 kilometers
0   200 miles

NEW
HAMPSHIRE

VERMONT

MAINE

MASSACHUSETTS

NEW
YORK

RHODE
ISLAND

CONNECTICU

PENNSYLVANIA

NEW
JERSEY

NORTH
DAKOTA

MINNESOTA

OHIO

DELAWARE

Washington, D.

MARYLAND

WEST
VIRGINIA

WISCONSIN

MICHIGAN

SOUTH
DAKOTA

IOWA

INDIANA

VIRGINIA

NEBRASKA

ILLINOIS

KENTUCKY

NORTH
CAROLINA

KANSAS

MISSOURI

TENNESSEE

SOUTH
CAROLINA

OKLAHOMA

ARKANSAS

GEORGIA

ALABAMA

TEXAS

MISSISSIPPI

LOUISIANA

FLORIDA

0   125   250 kilometers

0   125   250 miles

R19

Picture Glossary

A

aid

Help to others is a kind of **aid**. (p. 322) The United States often sends **aid** to countries where an earthquake has struck.

ancestor

A family member who lived before you is an **ancestor.** (p. 120) An **ancestor** of mine lived in China in the 1600s.

B

ballot

A **ballot** is a form on which people mark their choices in an election. (p. 311) Many communities have switched from paper **ballots** to voting machines.

bank

A **bank** is a safe place to keep money. (p. 181) Dad went to the **bank** to get money for gas.

bar graph

A **bar graph** is a chart that uses bars to show amounts. (p. 178) The **bar graph** shows the number of different workers in a school.

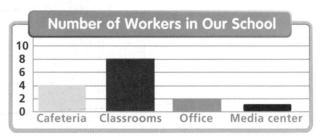

Number of Workers in Our School

| | Cafeteria | Classrooms | Office | Media center |

barter

The exchange of goods or services without the use of money is called **barter.** (p. 196) **Barter** takes place when you swap goods or services with someone.

calendar

A **calendar** is a chart that shows the months, weeks, and days of the year. (p. 50) I marked my birthday on the **calendar.**

capital

A **capital** is a city where the people in a government work. (p. 284) The **capital** of New Jersey is Trenton.

capital resource

Something other than natural or human resources, that people need in order to produce goods is a **capital resource.** (p. 191) **Capital resources** include tools, machinery, buildings, and trucks.

cause

A **cause** is something that makes something else happen. (p. 238) The **cause** of the fire was a lightning strike.

citizen

A **citizen** is a person who belongs to a place. (p. 292) You are a **citizen** of the community where you live.

climate

The usual weather of a place over a long time is called **climate.** (p. 85) Southern Michigan has a **climate** with cold winters and warm summers.

colonist

A **colonist** is a person who lives in a colony. (p. 230) The **colonists** at Jamestown came from England.

colony

A **colony** is a place that is ruled by another country. (p. 229) England's first **colony** in North America was Jamestown.

communication

Any way of sharing information is **communication.** (p. 268) Newspapers and magazines are kinds of **communication.**

community

A **community** is a place where people live. (p. 38) Cities and towns are **communities.**

compass rose

A **compass rose** is a drawing that shows directions on a map. (p. 34) Use the **compass rose** to find north.

conflict

A **conflict** is a disagreement. (p. 314) Good citizens try to resolve **conflicts** peacefully.

Constitution

The **Constitution** is a plan for the government of the United States. (p. 316) The United States **Constitution** is more than 200 years old.

consumer

A **consumer** is someone who buys or uses goods or services. (p. 166) I am a **consumer** when I buy food at a store.

continent

A **continent** is a large body of land. (p. 68) The earth has seven **continents.**

country

A **country** is a land where people have the same laws and leaders. (p. 67) Mexico is the **country** south of the United States.

culture

The way of life of a group of people is called **culture.** (p. 117) Religious beliefs are part of people's **culture.**

custom

A **custom** is a ceremony or special activity

shared among groups of people. (p. 116) It is our **custom** to wear party hats at birthday parties.

decision

A **decision** is the act of deciding or of making a choice. (p. 150)

I had to make a **decision** about doing my homework before or after supper.

democracy

A **democracy** is government by the people. (p. 317) People

in a **democracy** choose their leaders.

detail

A **detail** is a small piece of information. (p. 98) Make sure you support your idea with **details.**

Main Idea
Details
1.
2.
3.
4.
5.

dictionary

A **dictionary** is a book that gives the meanings of words. (p. 186) Look up new words in a **dictionary.**

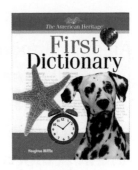

distance

The word **distance** means how far one point is from another.

(p. 202) The **distance** across the table is 30 inches.

effect

An **effect** is

cause	→	effect

something that happens as a result of a cause. (p. 238) An **effect** of playing in puddles is wet clothing.

election

An **election** is a time when people vote. (p. 308) We have an **election**

to choose a new President every four years.

encyclopedia

An **encyclopedia** is a book or set of books that gives information about many topics. (p. 186) Look up a topic in an **encyclopedia** to find out more about it.

environment

The **environment** is the natural world around you. (p. 103) Land, water, plants, animals, and people are all part of the **environment.**

equator

The **equator** is an imaginary line that divides the earth into its northern and southern halves. (p. 72) You can only see the **equator** on maps.

explorer

An **explorer** is a person who travels to find new things and places. (p. 222) Columbus was an **explorer** who traveled to the Americas.

 F

fact

A **fact** is something that is true. (pp. 164, 250) A book about seashells has many **facts** in it.

factory

A **factory** is a place where goods are made. (p. 172) It would be fun to go to a sneaker **factory.**

fiction

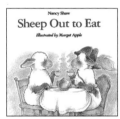

Written works that tell about made-up events and characters are called **fiction.** (p. 164) The stories "Cinderella" and **Sheep Out to Eat** are **fiction.**

G

globe

A **globe** is a ball-shaped model of the earth. (p. 32) A **globe** shows the true shape of the earth.

goods

Things people make or grow are called **goods**.
(p. 172) Goods are things such as trucks and apples.

government

A group of people who work together to run a community, state, or country make up a **government**. (p. 283)
Some people in our **government** work at city hall.

grid

A **grid** is a pattern of lines that form boxes. (p. 42) A **grid** helps you find places on a map.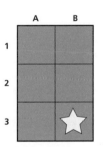

group

A **group** is a number of people who live together, work together, or
spend time together. (p. 26) A soccer team is a **group**.

hemisphere

A **hemisphere** is half the earth. (p. 72) North America is in the Western **Hemisphere**.

hero

A **hero** is someone who is admired for great courage or for doing something important. (p. 252)
Heroes can be found in medicine, sports, science, or other areas.

history

Everything people can know about the past is called **history**. (p. 212) The invention of
the computer was an important event in **history**.

human resource

A **human resource** is a person who helps make a product. (p. 190)
A worker in a factory or other places is a **human resource**.

immigrant

An **immigrant** is a person who moves from one country to another. (p. 118) In the 1970s, many **immigrants** came to the United States from Asia.

income

The money people earn when they work is called **income.** (p. 168) My mother uses her **income** to pay for our food.

independence

Independence means freedom from the rule of another nation. (p. 242) The 13 colonies wanted **independence** from Britain.

interview

An **interview** is a meeting in which one person asks another person questions. (p. 134) In our **interview** with the mayor, we asked five questions.

invention

An **invention** is something new that someone makes or thinks of. (p. 256) Thomas Edison thought of many important **inventions.**

island

An **island** is a piece of land with water all around it. (p. 76) Greenland is a very large **island.**

J

journey

A **journey** is a long trip. (p. 222) Colonists from England made a **journey** from Europe to North America.

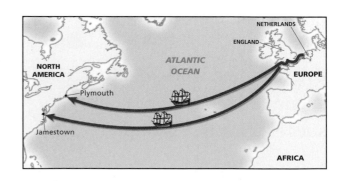

judge

A **judge** is someone who studies the laws and decides the best way to follow them. (p. 302) A **judge** may decide what a person must do to make up for breaking a law.

justice

Justice means fairness. (p. 317) A good judge treats everyone with **justice.**

lake

A body of water with land all around it is called a **lake.** (p. 78) Most **lakes** have fresh water.

landform

A **landform** is one of the shapes of land found on the earth. (p. 74) A mountain is a **landform.**

landmark

A **landmark** is something that helps people know a place. (p. 138) The Gateway Arch is a **landmark** of St. Louis, Missouri.

law

A rule that everyone in a community, state, or nation must follow is called a **law.** (p. 300) A driver who doesn't stop at a stop sign is breaking a **law.**

leader

A **leader** is someone who leads others. (p. 28) A community **leader** guides the work of others.

legend

A **legend** is a story that people have passed along for many years. (p. 128) Most cultures have a **legend** that explains weather.

liberty

The word **liberty** means freedom. (p. 317) The **Liberty** Bell is a symbol of our nation's freedom.

location

A **location** is a place. (p. 42) An airplane symbol may mark the **location** of an airport on a map.

main idea

The most important thought on a page is called a **main idea.** (p. 98) The **main idea** on that page is that people have many kinds of pets.

market

A **market** is any place where people buy and sell things. (p. 55) A small store is one kind of **market.**

memorial

A **memorial** is something, such as a building or statue, that honors a hero or an event. (p. 140) The Vietnam Veterans **Memorial** honors Americans who were killed in the Vietnam War.

monument

A **monument** is something, such as a building or statue, that honors a hero or an event. (p. 140) Many towns have a **monument** to people who served in a war.

nation

Nation is another word for country. (p. 68) Canada is a **nation** to the north of the United States.

national holiday

A **national holiday** is a holiday that honors someone or something that is important to a country. (p. 144) Independence Day is a **national holiday** that honors the beginning of the United States.

natural resource

Something in nature that people use is a **natural resource.** (p. 100) Water is an important **natural resource.**

needs

Things that people must have to live are called **needs.** (p. 160) Our **needs** are food, water, clothing, and shelter.

neighborhood

A neighborhood is a part of a city or town. (p. 36) Each year, people in my **neighborhood** get together for a picnic on Labor Day.

nonfiction

Written materials that are about true things are **nonfiction.** (p. 164) **Sheep on the Farm** is a **nonfiction** book.

northeast

The direction between north and east is called **northeast.** (p. 82) New York City is **northeast** of Trenton, New Jersey.

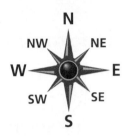

northwest

The direction between north and west is called **northwest.** (p. 82) Montgomery, Alabama is **northwest** of Tallahassee, Florida.

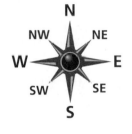

opinion

An **opinion** is a belief based on what you think or feel, rather than on facts. (p. 250) In my **opinion** soccer is better than baseball.

peninsula

Land that sticks out into water is called a **peninsula.** (p. 76) A **peninsula** has water on three sides.

pictograph

A **pictograph** is a chart that shows information by using small pictures to stand for amounts. (p. 306) Each picture of a tomato can on the **pictograph** stood for ten tomatoes.

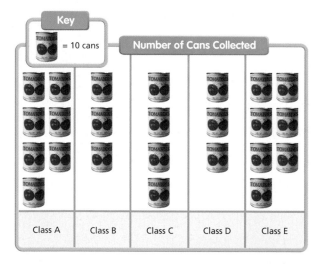

Key

= 10 cans   Number of Cans Collected

Class A   Class B   Class C   Class D   Class E

Pilgrim

A **Pilgrim** was one kind of colonist at Plymouth. (p. 232) The **Pilgrims** came to America to find religious freedom.

point of view

A way of looking at things is called a **point of view.** (p. 266) We each had a different **point of view** about which play to put on.

pole

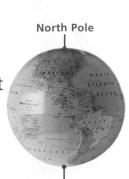

North Pole

South Pole

The place on the earth that is farthest north or south is a kind of **pole.** (p. 72) The North **Pole** and the South **Pole** are very cold.

president

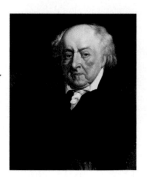

A **president** is the leader of a country or nation. (p. 138) John Adams was the second **President** of the United States.

price

The amount of money you pay to buy something is called **price.** (p. 180) The **price** of a box of cereal is $2.79.

Picture Glossary

producer

A **producer** is a person who makes or grows something. (p. 166) A baker is a **producer** of bread and rolls.

region

A **region** is an area that has some shared natural or human feature that sets it apart from other areas. (p. 92) The state of Iowa is in a plains **region.**

religious holiday

A special day that is important to people in a religion is called a **religious holiday.** (p. 146) In April, Buddhists celebrate the birthday of their founder on a **religious holiday** called Wesak.

responsibility

A **responsibility** is something that you should do. (p. 294) Everyone has the **responsibility** to obey the law.

right

A **right** is something you are free to do. (p. 293) You have the **right** to speak freely.

rule

A statement or an idea that tells people what they should or should not do is called a **rule.** (p. 29) One school **rule** says that you may not run in the hallway.

rural area

A **rural** area is a place that has fewer stores, schools, and homes than a city or suburb has. (p. 53) Farms and forests are found in **rural areas.**

savings account

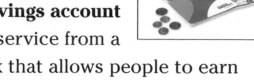

A **savings account** is a service from a bank that allows people to earn interest on their money. (p. 182) Aki's **savings account** earned 11 cents in interest last month.

scale

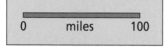

A line with a series of marks used to find distance on a map is a **scale.** (p. 202) Use a map **scale** to find how far apart two places are.

scarcity

Not having enough resources to meet people's unlimited wants is called **scarcity.** Because of scarcity, people must make choices in what to make or grow. (p. 193)

service

An activity that people do to help other people is called a **service.** (p. 173) A dentist provides a **service.**

settlement

A **settlement** is a small community started by people from another land. (p. 229) St. Augustine in Florida is the oldest lasting European **settlement** in America.

shelter

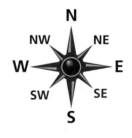

Something that protects or covers is called a **shelter.** (p. 160) Houses are kinds of **shelter.**

southeast

The direction between south and east is called **southeast.** (p. 82) Springfield, Illinois, is **southeast** of Des Moines, Iowa.

southwest

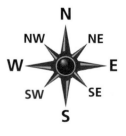

The direction between south and west is called **southwest.** (p. 82) Frankfort, Kentucky is **southwest** of Columbus, Ohio.

specialize

Choosing to grow mainly one crop or to make only one main kind of product is to **specialize.** (p. 199) Farmers in Costa Rica **specialize** in growing bananas.

state

Part of a country is called a **state.** (p. 67) Ohio is one **state** of the 50 in the United States.

suburb

A **suburb** is a community near a city. (p. 46) Many people who live in a **suburb** work in the city.

symbol

A **symbol** is a picture, place, or thing that stands for something else. (pp. 34, 137) An eagle is a **symbol** of freedom.

tax

A **tax** is money that a government collects from citizens and businesses. (p. 287) A local government uses the **tax** money it collects to pay for services such as police.

technology

The use of science to make new things or to make things work better is called **technology.** (p. 260) People used **technology** to make faster and safer cars.

timeline

A **timeline** is an ordered group of words and dates that show when events happened. (p. 124) A **timeline** must be divided into equal parts.

Dan's Life History

Dan was born   Dan learned to read   Dan today

trade

The buying and selling of goods and services is called **trade.** (p. 197) People in this country take part in **trade** in many ways.

tradition

A **tradition** is something that people do the same way year after year. (p. 126) One **tradition** in my family is that you choose what is served for dinner on your birthday.

transportation

Any way of moving things or people from one place to another is called **transportation.** (p. 260) Cars are one kind of **transportation.**

urban area

Urban area is another name for city. (p. 44) An **urban area** has many buildings and people.

valley

The low land between mountains or hills is called a **valley.** (p. 75) A **valley** often has a river running through it.

vote

To **vote** means to show or make a choice for a leader or a law. (p. 308) You may **vote** for class president or team captain.

wants

Things that people would like to have, but do not have to have to stay alive are called **wants.** (p. 160) A new bike and roller skates are on my list of **wants.**

weather

What the air is like outside at any given time is called **weather.** (p. 84) Today the **weather** is warm and rainy.

world map

A **world map** is a flat drawing of the earth. (p. 32) You can see the whole earth at once on a **world map.**

Index

Page numbers with "m" after them refer to maps. Page numbers in italics refer to pictures.

Absolute location, 34–35, 42, 60

Adame-Moliner, Alicia, 130

Adams, Abigail, 245–247

Adams, Samuel, 245

Address, in geography, 66

Aid, definition of, 322

African Americans
Carver, George Washington, 176
civil rights and, 293, 304–305, 334
inventors, 176, 264
Martin Luther King, Jr., Day, 334
Parks, Rosa, 304–305, R8
Robinson, Jackie, 255, 258–259
Woods, Granville T., 264

Agriculture. *See* Farms and farming.

American Indians, 118–119
canoes, 217
Cherokee, 80–81
Delaware, 213m–214
"Great Smokies, The," 80–81
history of, 213–215
legends, 218–221
natural resources, 216
Navajo, 213m, 214, 216
Osage, 213m, 215–216
Pamunkey, 230
powwows, 119
Shasta, 213m, 215
Sitting Bull, 253
totem poles, 129
Wampanoag, 232

American Revolution
causes, 242
events, 243–244
leaders of, 244–249
people, 242–249

Ancestors, 120–121

Appalachian Mountains, 83

Arafat, Yasir, 325

Art and artists, 129–131

Artifacts, 139, 209, 216, 217, 226, 243, 247, 258, 269–272, 281, 316, 332, 334

Australia, 201, R13m, R15m

Ballots, 311–313

Banks, 181
savings accounts, 182–183

Bar graphs, 178–179

Barter, 196

Begin, Menachem, 323

Bell, Alexander Graham, 269

Blair, Tony, 325

Boston, Massachusetts, 241

Boston Tea Party, 242

Branches of government, 318–319

Brazil, money of, 200

Bush, George W., 324

Buyers, 56–57

Calendars, reading, 50–51

California
capital resources, 191
Central Valley, 53
Cesar Chavez Day of Service and Learning, 145
Chavez, Cesar, 148–149
Chula Vista, 47m
climate, 83
crops, 53, 87, 190, 192
farming, 53, 83, 190, 192–193
farm labor movement, 148–149
human resources, 190
Lake Tahoe, 78
landforms, 77
land use, 55
Long Beach Airport, 206
Los Angeles, 83m
mayors, 280
natural resources, 190
Pacific Ocean, 83m
Palm Springs, 86–87
Sacramento, 38
San Bernardino, 44
San Diego, 46–47
San Diego Zoo, 47
Santa Rosa, 35m
Santee, 47m
Shasta, 213m, 215
Sierra Nevada, 74m, 83m
Spring Valley, 46–47m
water, 193
Yosemite Valley, 75

Canada, 69

Capital resources, 191. *See also* Resources.

Capitals, 284

Capitol, definition of, 319

Caring, 174–177, R9

Index

Carter, Jimmy, 323

Carver, George Washington, 176

Cause and effect, 44, 196, 238–239, 338–339

Cent, 200–201

Centavo, 200

Central Valley, California, 53

Cervantes, Maggie, 40–41

Cesar Chavez Day of Service and Learning, 145

Character traits, R8–R9
caring, 174–177, R9
civic virtue, 40–41, 295, R9
courage, 304–305, R8–R9
fairness, 148–149, 317, R9
patriotism, 246–249, R8–R9
respect, 258–259, R9
responsibility, 296–299, R9

Charleston, South Carolina, 241

Chavez, Cesar, 148–149

Cherokee
folklore of, 80–81

Chicago, Illinois, 45

Chinese New Year, 118

Choices, economic, 161

Chula Vista, California, 47m

Cities, 44–45, 58
characteristics of, 44–45
as communities, 38
neighborhoods, 36
parks, 38m, 44

Citizens, 292
definition of, 280, 292, 329
elections, 309–311
equality, 293
good citizens, 295
government, 293, 309–311
laws and, 303

responsibilities of, 294, 296–299
rights of, 293, 295
voting and, 311

Citizenship
civic understanding, 40–41, 294, 295, R9
civic virtue, 40–41, 295, R9
Constitution, 316–318
democracy, 317, 320–321
elections, 308–313
government defined, 283
judges, 302
laws, 300–305
leaders, 308–311
police, 301
responsibilities, 294, 296–299
rights, 293, 295

Citizenship Handbook, R2–R9

Citizenship skills, 150–151, 266–267, 314–315

Civic virtue, 40–41, 295, R9

Climate, 85–87. *See also* Weather.

Colonies, 229, 240–241m
American Revolution, 244
colonists, 230
Declaration of Independence, 243
Jamestown, 229m, 230–231
Plymouth, 229m, 232–233

Colorado River, 67, 83

Columbus, Christopher, 224–225

Communication, 268
Inca messengers, 272–273
Internet, 271
radio, 270
stagecoach mail, 268
telegraph, 269
telephone, 269
television, 270

Communities, 38–40

Community activities, 39

Compare and contrast. *See* Reading Skills.

Compasses, 226–227

Compass rose, 34

Conflict resolution, 296–299, 314–315

Congress, 319

Constitution of the United States, 316–317
branches of government and, 318–319

Consumers, 166–167, 204

Continents, 68–69

Country, definition of, 67

Courage, 304–305, R8–R9

Critical thinking
cause and effect, 238–239
classify, 153
compare and contrast, 59, 109
conflict resolution, 296–299, 314–315
decision making, 150–151
main idea and details, 205
sequence, 275

Culture
art, 129
customs, 116–117
dance and, 130–131
families and, 117
from ancestors, 120–121
holidays and, 144–148
immigrants, 118–123
landmarks, 138–139
language, 117
literature and, 128
monuments, 140–141
music and, 130–131
sharing, 126–131
stories, 128

Culture
  symbols, 118–119, 136
  traditions from, 126–127
  United States, 136
Curie, Marie, 174
Customs, 116–117

Decision making, 150–151
Declaration of Independence, 243
Delaware Indians, 213m–214
Delaware River, 79
  George Washington crossing, 244
Delmarva Peninsula, 76
Democracy, 320–321
Democratic ideals,
  freedom, 317, 338
  justice, 317
Dictionaries, using, 186–187
Directions, geography, 82
Distance measurement on a map, 202
Documents, 120–121, 243, 258–259, 316–317
Dollar, 201
Drew, Charles, 252
Duluth, Minnesota, 284–285m

Earning money, 168
Easter, 146. *See also* Holidays.
Economics
  banks, 181–183
  barter, 196
  buyers and sellers, 56–57
  capital resources, 191

  choices, 161, 180, 184–185, 193
  comparing prices, 184–185
  consumers, 166–167, 204
  exchange, 196–200
  free enterprise, 192–193
  goods, 172
  human resources, 190
  income, 168
  interdependence of consumers and producers, 166–167, 198–199
  interest, 182
  markets, 55–57
  money, 168, 181, 200–201
  needs, 160, 162–163
  opportunity cost, 161
  price, 180
  producers, 166–167, 170–171, 204
  saving, 181–183
  savings accounts, 182–183
  scarcity, 192–193
  services, 173–177
  specialization, 199
  trade, 197–198
  wants, 160
Edison, Thomas, 256
Einstein, Albert, 257
Elections, 308–313
Electric light bulb, 256
Ellis Island, New York, 122–123
Encyclopedias, 186
English colonies, 229, 240–241m
  American Revolution, 244
  Declaration of Independence, 243
  Jamestown, 229m–231
  Plymouth, 229m, 232–233

Environment, 103
  harm to, 104–105
  protection of, 104–105
Equator, 72
European Union
  money of, 200
Explorers, 222, 228
  Christopher Columbus, 224–225
  Marco Polo, 222–223

Fact and fiction, comparing, 164
Fact and opinion, comparing, 250
Factories, 172
Fairness, 148–149, 317, R9
Families
  ancestors, 120–121
  cultures and, 117
  customs, 116
  groups, 26–27
  sharing traditions, 126–127
  tracing history of, 124–125
Fargo, North Dakota, 86
Farm labor movement, 148–149
Farms and farming
  first farmers, 170–171
  in Mesopotamia, 170–171
  producers, 166, 188–189
  raisin production, 188–191
  rural areas and, 53
  specializing in, 199
Fire fighters, 288–291
Fish markets, 57
Flag Day, 337
Flags
  Ghana, 327

Index

Japan, 327

Mexico, 326

United States, 136–137

Florida, 38–39

Folktales

"Fox and the Crab, The," 128

"Great Smokies, The," 80–81

"Milkmaid, The," 162–163

"Young Woman and the Thunder Beings, The," 218–221

Food

distributors, 197

keeping cold (refrigeration), 194–195

processors, 190

timeline, 194–195

Forest regions, 94

Forests, 54, 95

Fort McHenry, 142

Fourth of July, 338

Franklin, Benjamin, 245, 268

Freedom, 317, 338

Free enterprise, 192–193

Geography, 66–107

climate, 85–87

community types, 46–47

continent, 68–69

country, 66–67

environment, 103–105

environmental modification, 102–105

human characteristics, 92, 96–97

human regions, 92, 96–97

landforms, 74–77

location, 66–69

nation, 69

natural resources, 100

nonrenewable resources, 102

physical characteristics, 92–95

regions, 92–97

renewable resources, 102

resources, 100–107

states, 67

water, bodies of, 78–79

weather, 84–85, 88–91

Globes, 32–33

parts of, 72–73

Goods, 172

Government

branches of, 318–319

institutions, 284, 286, 301–302

leaders, 308–310

local, 283

national, 284

services, 286

state, 284

taxes, 287

working together, 323

world leaders, 323–325

Governors, 309

Graph and chart skills, 124–125, 150–151, 178–179, 306–307

Grassland regions, 94

Great Lakes, 78, 83

"Great Smokies, The," 80–81

Grids, and map location, 42–43

Groups, 26–27

individual actions within, 26–27

leaders, 28

rules, 29

Gulf of Mexico, 83

Hawaii forest, 95

Hemispheres, 72

Heroes, 252–257

Hezekiah, Alan, 130

Highways, 263

History

American Indians, 212–217

American Revolution, 242–249

changes over time, 260–263

colonists, 230–233, 240–243

communication changes, 268–271

Constitution of the United States, 316–319

Declaration of Independence, 243

explorers, 222–225

heroes, 252–257

inventions, 227, 262—265, 268–271

Jamestown, 230–231

Plymouth, 232–233

timelines, 124–125, 154, 194–195, 242–243, 246, 248, 262–263, 274

transportation changes, 264–265

Holidays

Cesar Chavez Day of Service and Learning, 145, 148

cultural holidays, 147

Flag Day, 337

Independence Day, 338

Martin Luther King, Jr., Day, 334

Memorial Day, 336

Holidays

national holidays, 144
Patriots' Day, 145
Presidents' Day, 144, 335
religious holidays, 146
state holidays, 145
Thanksgiving, 333
Veterans Day, 332
Human regions, 92
Human resources, 190–191

Immigrants
ancestors and, 120–121
definition of, 118
at Ellis Island, New York, 122–123
Inca message runners, 272–273
Income, 168
Independence, 242
American Revolution, 244
Declaration of Independence, 243
leaders of, 245
Independence Day, 338
India, money of, 201
Interdependence, *of* consumers-producers, 166–167, 198–199
Intermediate directions, 82–83
Internet, 56, 271
Interviews, 134–135
Inventions, 256
in communications, 268–271
in transportation, 260–263
Islands, 76

Jamestown, 229–231
Japan, 326m

flag of, 327
market, 57
Jefferson, Thomas, 141, 243
Jefferson Memorial, 141
Judges, 302
Supreme Court, 319
Justice, 317

Kenya, 201m
money of, 200
Key, Francis Scott, 142
King, Martin Luther, Jr., 334

Lakes, 78, 83
Lake Superior, 78
Lake Tahoe, California, 78
Landform regions, 93
Landforms, 74
islands, 76
mountains, 75
peninsulas, 76
plains, 77
valleys, 75
Landmarks, 138–139
Liberty Bell, 139
Mount Rushmore, 138
Statue of Liberty, 139
Laws
citizens' obedience to, 303
environment and, 105
importance of, 300
judges and, 302
police and, 301
Leaders, 28
government, 308–311, 323–325
of independence, 245

Legends, 128, 218–221
Letters, as primary sources, 258–259
Liberty, 317
Liberty Bell, 139
Lincoln, Abraham
Lincoln Memorial, 140
Presidents' Day, 335
Literature
"Fire Station, The," 288–291
"Great Smokies, The," 80–81
"Maple Talk," 106–107
"Milkmaid, The," 162–163
"Recess Rules," 30–31
"Star-Spangled Banner, The," 142–143
"Young Woman and the Thunder Beings, The," 218–221
Local government, 283
mayors, 309
services, 286
taxes, 286
Location
absolute, 34–35, 42, 60
on grid, 42
relative, 34–35, 82–83, 202–203
Longhouses, 214–215
Los Angeles, California, 83m

Magnetic compasses, 226–227
Mail, by stagecoach, 268
Mandela, Nelson, 325
Map and globe skills, 32–35, 42–43, 72–73, 82–83, 202–203
Map key, 34–35
"Maple Talk," 106–107

Index

Maps
American Indian groups, 213m
ancestors, 120m
Brown Elementary School, 60m
colonies, thirteen, 241m
Columbus's first journey, 224m
continents, 68m, R12m–R13m
Eastern United States, 203m
Europe to Asia, route, 223m
Fargo, North Dakota, 86m
Florida, 76m
Ghana, 326m
globe, 110m
grid, 43m
Havre, Montana, 118m
hemispheres, 73m
Inca homelands, 272m
Israel, 254m
Japan, 326m
Lakota, 253m
landform regions, United States, 93m
landmarks, United States, 138m
Long Beach Airport, 206m
Massachusetts, 78m
Mayflower, route, 229m
Mesopotamia, 170m
Mexico, 326m
money, world, 201m
Nebraska, 77m
New York City, 118m
North America, 69m, R16m–R17m
North America, land and water, 108m
North Pole, 32m
Oregon, 75m
Palm Springs, California, 86m
Pittsburgh, Pennsylvania, 79m
Plainfield, Illinois, 1873 and Today, 261m
plant regions, United States, 94m
rainfall, United States, 99m
Sacramento, California, 38m
San Diego, California, 47m
San Francisco, California, 118m
Santa Rosa, California, 35m
Sierra Nevada, 74m
South Pole, 32m
southwestern states, 110m
Spring Valley, California, 47m
Switzerland, languages, 97m
trade, bananas and wheat, 198m
United States, 67m, 83m, 284m–285m, R18m–R19m
world, 33m, 201m, R14m–R15m
world, physical, R14m–R15m
world leaders, 324m
See also Skills: Map and Globe.
Map scale, 202
Maps of the world, 32–33, 201m, R14m–R15m
Marco Polo, 222–223
Markets, 55–57
Marrakesh market, 56
Martin Luther King, Jr., Day, 334
"Mayflower Crossing, The," 234–237

Mayors, 309
Meir, Golda, 254
Memorial Day, 336
Memorials, 140–141
Lincoln Memorial, 140
Thomas Jefferson Memorial, 141
Mesopotamia, 170
Message runners, 272–273
Mexico, 69
flag, 326
music and dancing, 131
"Milkmaid, The," 162–163. *See also* Folktales.
Mississippi River, 83, R14
Missouri River, 63, 83
Money
Australia, 201
Brazil, 200
earning money, 162–163, 168
European Union, 200
India, 201
Jordan, 200
Kenya, 200
saving money, 181
United States, 200
Monuments, 140
Morse, Samuel, 269
Mountains, 74–75, 80, 83m, 93m
Mount Rushmore, 138
Musical traditions, 130, 133

National anthem, 142–143
National government, 284
branches of government, 318–319
Constitution of the United States, 316–317
President of the United States, 138, 309, 318

services, 286
National holidays, 144
Flag Day, 337
Independence Day, 338
Martin Luther King, Jr.,
Day, 334
Memorial Day, 336
Presidents' Day, 335
Thanksgiving, 333
Veterans Day, 332
Nations, 69
flags of, 326–327
working together, 322–325
Native Americans, 118, 119
canoes, 217
Cherokee, folklore of,
80–81
Delaware, 213m–214
"Great Smokies, The,"
80–81
history of, 213–215
legends, 218–221
natural resources, use of,
216
Navajo, 213m, 214, 216
Osage, 213m, 215–216
Pamunkey, 230
powwows, 119
Shasta, 213m, 215
Sitting Bull, 253
totem poles, 129
Wampanoag, 232
Natural resources, 100, 191
American Indians' use of,
216
raisin producers, 190
replacement of, 102
Navajo, 213m, 214, 216
Needs, definition of, 160,
162–163
Neighborhood activities,
37
Neighborhoods, 36. *See*

also Communities.
New England forest, 95
New York City, 48–49
immigrants, 119
Nonfiction, definition of,
164
North America, 69, 108,
R16–R17m
Northeast, 82
North Pole, 72
Northwest, 82

Ocean water, 78
Oil, replacement of, 102
Opinion and fact, 250
Opportunity cost, 161
Origami, 127
Osage, 213m, 215–216

Pacific Ocean, 69
Palm Springs, California,
86–87
Pamunkey, 230
Parades, holiday, *145, 147*
Parks, Rosa, 304–305, R8
Passover, 146
Pasteur, Louis, 175. *See
also* Scientists.
Pasteurization, 175
Patriotism, 246–249, R8, R9
Patriots' Day, 145
Peninsulas, 76
Philadelphia, 241
Liberty Bell, 139
Pictographs, 306–307
Pilgrims, 232
"Mayflower Crossing,
The," 234–237
in Plymouth Colony,
232–233

Plainfield, Illinois, 261–263
Plains, 77
Plant regions, 94–95
Plymouth Colony, 229m,
232–233
Police, 301
Polo, Marco, 222–223
Powwows, 119
Presidents' Day, 335
**Presidents of the United
States,** 138, 309, 318
Bush, George W., 324
Carter, Jimmy, 323
Jefferson, Thomas, 141, 243
Lincoln, Abraham, 140,
335
seal of the President, 136
Washington, George, 140,
335
Price, 180
comparing, 184–185
Primary sources, 22, 41, 62,
71, 80, 112, *116*–119,
120–121, *122–127,*
130–131, 134, 143, 148,
156, 208, 218–221, 233,
243, 247, 258–259, 278,
316, R2, R4, R6–R7
Problem-solving, 296–299
Producers, 166–167,
170–171, 204
raisin production, 188–191
Putin, Vladimir, 324

Radios, 270
Railways, 262
Rainfall, in the United
States, 99
Raisin production, 188–191
Ramadan, 146
Readers' Theater, 88–91,
234–237, 296–299
Reading skills

cause and effect, 44, 196

classify, 66, 136, 144, 172, 212, 252, 292, 316

compare and contrast, 26, 52, 74, 222, 228

draw conclusions, 116, 166, 282

fact and opinion, 250–251

main idea and details, 36, 84, 92, 98, 126, 268, 300

predict outcomes, 160, 180

problem and solution, 314–315, 322

sequence, 100, 188, 240, 260, 308

Reading strategies

monitor and clarify, 65, 211

predict and infer, 25, 115, 211

question, 65, 159, 281

summarize, 25, 115, 159, 281

"Recess Rules," 30–31

Recycling, 105

Regions, 92, 96

human regions, 92, 96–97

landform regions, 93

plant regions, 94–95

Relative location, 34–35, 82–83, 202–203

Religious holidays, 146

Resources, 100

capital resources, 191

human resources, 190–191

natural resources, 100, 102, 190, 191, 216

scarcity of, 192–193

water resources, 78–79, 100, 105

Respect, 258–259, R9

Responsibilities, citizens and, 294, 296–299

Responsibility, character trait, 296–299, R9

Revere, Paul, 245, 248–249

Revolutionary War. *See* American Revolution.

Rickey, Branch, 258–259

Ride, Sally, 70–71

Rights, 293

of African Americans, 255, 258–259, 293, 304–305, 334, R8

of American Indians, 253, 293

of Mexican Americans, 148–149

of women, 40–41, 70, 254, 293

Rivers, 79

Robinson, Jackie, 255, 258–259

Rocky Mountains, 83

Rodriguez, Eloy, 177

Rules, 29

"Recess Rules," 30–31

Rural areas, 53

Sacramento, California, 38, 44

Sadat, Anwar el–, 323

Safety

"Recess Rules," 30–31

Saint Patrick's Day parade, 147

San Bernardino, California, 44

San Diego, California, 47

Spring Valley suburb, 46

San Diego Zoo, 47

Santa Rosa, California, 35m

Santee, California, 47m

Saving money, 181

Savings accounts, 182–183

Scarcity, of resources, 192–193

School class, 26–27

Scientists, 174–177

Secondary sources, 40–41, 70–71, 130–131, 148–149, 174–177, 186–187, 246, 264–265, 304–305

Sellers, 56–57

Seneca

legends, 218–221

Sequence of events, 242–243, 246, 248, 262–263, 274

Services, 173

government services, 286

Settlements, 229

Jamestown, 229m–231

Plymouth, 229m, 232–233

Shasta, 213m, 215

Shelter, 160

Sitting Bull, 253

Skills

citizenship

conflict resolution, 314–315

decision making, 150–151

point of view, 266–267

graph and chart

bar graph, 178–179

calendar, 50–51

pictograph, 306–307

timeline, 122–125

map and globe

compass rose, 34–35

globe, 32, 72–73

grid, 42–43

intermediate directions, 82–83

map scale, 202–203

symbols, 34–35

reading and thinking

Index

cause and effect, 238–239

facts and opinions, 250–251

study

fact and fiction, 164–165

interviewing, 134–135

main idea and details, 98–99

reference books, 186–187

Skyscrapers, 49

Small towns, 52

Soil loss, 104

Southeast, 82

South Pole, 72

Southwest, 82

Space shuttle science lab, 265

Specialization, 199

Spring Valley, California, 46–47m

Stagecoaches, 262

mail by, 268

"Star-Spangled Banner, The," 142–143

State

capitals, 284

definition of, 67

government, 284

governors, 309

holidays, 145, 148

laws, 300–301, 303–304

services, 286

United States, 66–67, 203m, 284–285m, R18–R19m

Statue of Liberty, 139

Story sharing, 128. *See also* Literature.

Streetcars, 262

Study skills, 186–187, 238–239

Suburbs, 46–47

Supreme Court, 319

Switzerland, languages of, 96–97

Symbols, 34, 137

American symbols, 136–137

Taxes, 287

Teams, as groups, 26

Technology, 260

Telegraph, 269

Railway Telegraph, 264

Woods, Granville T., 264

Telephone, 269

Television, 270

Thanksgiving, 333

Thomas Jefferson Memorial, 141

Timelines, 124–125, 154, 194–195, 242–243, 246, 248, 262–263, 274

Totem poles, 129

Towns

as communities, 38

neighborhoods, 36

small towns, 52

Trade, 197–198

Traditions, 126–127

Transportation, 260

cars, 263

highways, 263

Plainfield, Illinois, 262–263

railways, 262

stagecoach, 262

streetcars, 262

Trees

conservation and, 104

logs, 54

lumber, 54, 104

honey mesquite, 98

"Maple Talk," 106–107

replacement of, 102

Uncle Sam, 137

United States Constitution, 316–317

branches of government and, 318–319

United States of America, 67, 244, 284–285m, R18–R19

Urban areas, 44, 47, 49, 55

Valleys, 75

Veterans Day, 332

Vietnam Veterans Memorial, 336

Voting, 308–313

Wampanoag, 232

Wang, Taylor G., 265

Wants, definition of, 160

War for Independence. *See* American Revolution.

Washington, D.C., 284

Washington, George

crossing the Delaware River, 244

Presidents' Day, 144

Washington Monument, 140

Water, bodies of, 78–79

Waters, in California, 193

Weather, 84

Weather reports, 84

Wheat, 198

White House, 318

Women in history, 40–41, 70–71, 174, 246–247, 304–305

Women's rights, 40–41, 70, 246–247, 254

Woods, Granville T., 264

Work, 166–169

World leaders, 323–325

World maps, 32–33

Index

Yosemite Valley, 75
"Young Woman and the Thunder Beings, The," 218–221
Yo-Yo Ma, 132–133

Zemin, Jiang, 325

Primary Source References

The complete version of a literary or primary source excerpt is given below. In many cases, the works can be found through sources other than those referenced.

Page 22

For the song "I Live in a City": Reynolds, Malvina. *Another Country Heard From.* Washington, DC: Folkways Records, 1960.

Page 30

For the poem "Recess Rules": Shields, Carol Diggory. New York: Penguin, 1995.

Page 41

For the quote by Maggie Cervantes: Telgen, Diane and Kamp, Jim. *Notable Hispanic Women, 1st Ed.* Detroit, MI: Gale Research, Inc., 1993.

Page 62

For the poem "Renascence" by Edna St. Vincent Millay: Ellis, Norma Millay. *Collected Poems by Edna St. Vincent Millay.* New York: Harper & Brothers Publishers, 1956.

Page 71

For the quote by Sally Ride: Weissman, Paul; McFadden, Lucy-Ann; and Johnson, Torrence. *The Encyclopedia of the Solar System.* San Diego, CA: Academic Press, 1998.

Page 80

For the legend "The Great Smokies": Bruchac, Joseph. *Between Earth and Sky: Legends of Native American Sacred Places.* San Diego, CA: Harcourt Children's Books, 1996.

Page 106

For the poem "Maple Talk": Moore, Lilian. *Poems Have Roots.* New York: Simon & Schuster, 1997.

Page 112

For the poem "Our Family Comes from 'Round the World": Hoberman, Mary Ann. *Fathers, Mothers, Sisters, Brothers: A Collection of Family Poems.* New York: Puffin Books, 1993.

Pages 120–121

For the quote by Kumar Bloomstein: Interview conducted via phone by publisher, October 2003. For the quote by Isabel Taysin Carter: Interview conducted via phone by publisher, October 2003.

Pages 130–131

For the quote by Alan Hezekiah: Interview conducted via phone by publisher, October 2003. For the quote by Alicia Adame-Molinar: Interview conducted via phone by publisher, October 2003.

Page 143

For the complete lyrics to "The Star Spangled Banner": Key, Francis Scott. "The Star Spangled Banner," American Treasures of the Library of Congress. http://www.loc.gov/exhibits/treasures/

Page 148

For the quote by Cesar Chavez: State of California Official web site. *Quotes by Cesar Chavez.* http://www.goserv.ca.gov/ccd/quotes.asp

Page 156

For the poem "Dudley Market, 1827": Mee, Arthur, ed. *The King's England: Staffordshire.* South Yorkshire, UK: The King's England Press, 1937.

Page 208

For the song "America": U.S. Department of State: International Information Programs. "Symbols and Celebrations." http://usinfo.state.gov/usa/infousa/

Pages 218–221

For the legend "The Young Woman and the Thunder Beings": Bruchac, Joseph. *Between Earth and Sky: Legends of Native American Sacred Places.* San Diego, CA: Harcourt Children's Books, 1996.

Page 243

For the text of the Declaration of Independence: U.S. National Archives and Records Administration. "The Declaration of Independence: A Transcription" http://www.archives.gov/national_archives_experience/

Page 247

For the letter by Abigail Adams: *The Book of Abigail and John: Selected Letters of the Adams Family, 1762-1784.* Butterfield, L.H.; Friedlaender, Marc; and Kline, Mary-Jo, Eds. Cambridge, MA: Harvard University Press, 1976.

Page 259

For the letter by Jackie Robinson: The Library of Congress, Manuscript Division, Branch Rickey Papers. *Letter from Jackie Robinson to Branch Rickey,* 1950. http://memory.loc.gov/ammem/collections/robinson/

Page 278

For the song "America:" U.S. Department of State: International Information Programs. "Symbols and Celebrations." http://usinfo. state.gov/usa/infousa/

Page 316

For the text of the Declaration of Independence: U.S. National Archives and Records Administration. "The Declaration of Independence: A Transcription" http://www.archives.gov/national_archives_experience/

Page R2

For the "Pledge of Allegiance:" Anonymous. "The Pledge of Allegiance," *The Youth's Companion,* October 1892.

Pages R4, R6 and R7

For the songs "America the Beautiful," "America," and "God Bless America": U.S. Department of State: International Information Programs. "Symbols and Celebrations."http://usinfo.state. gov/usa/infousa/

Acknowledgments

Photography Credits

Cover (San Francisco) © Richard Cummins/CORBIS. (grass) © Royalty-Free/Corbis. (puppy digital composite) © David P. Hall/Masterfile. (newspaper digital composite) © Image source/Alamy Images. (stamps) AP/Wide World Photos. (map) © MAPS.com/CORBIS. (back cover) Peter Bennett/Ambient Images/Alamy Images. **22–23** Kwane Zikomo/Superstock. **24** Gibson Stock Photography. **25** (l) Wes Thompson/Corbis; (r) Claver Carroll/Botanica/Getty Images. **26** Arthur Tilley/Taxi/Getty Images. **28** (l) SW Productions/Photodisc Red/Getty Images; (r) Rhoda Sidney/Photo Edit, Inc. **39** (c) Digital DataStream Inc/Paint Your Heart Out Tampa; (tr) Richard Steinmetz. **40–41** Courtesy of Maggie Cervantes. **44** Robert Holmes Photography **45** (tl) Owaki–Kulla/Corbis; (tr) Gibson Stock Photography. **46** (lc) Mark Richards/Photo Edit; (tr) Stephen Schauer/Stone/Getty Images. **48** (inset) Brinsley Ford Collection, London, UK/Bridgeman Art Library. **48–49** (bkgd) Andrew Gordon 2003/Panoramic Images. **50** Mitch Hrdlicka/Photodisc Green/Getty Images. **52** J Sohm/VOA LLC/Panoramic Images. **53** Londie Padelsky/Index Stock Imagery. **54** (br) Jeff Green Berg/Photo Edit; (c) Alan Oddie/Photo Edit; (lc) Alec Pytlowany/Masterfile; (tr) Kitayama Sugi/Photonica. **55** (c) Rachel Epstein/Photo Edit; (inset) Richard Hamilton Smith/Corbis. **56** (b) David South/Image State–Pictor/PictureQuest; (t) Jon Riley Index Stock Imagery. **57** (l) TRBfoto/Photodisc/Getty Images; (r) TSUVOI/Masterfile. **62–63** (bkgd) Jesse Kalisher Gallery/Superstock; (inset) Palmer Kane Studios. **64** Mark Heifner/Pan Stock/Picturequest. **65** (l) Michael Melford/Imagebank/Getty Images;(r) Dan Budnik/Woodfin Camp & Associates. **70–71** (inset) NASA; (bkgd) Image produced by F. Hasler, M. Jentoft–Nilsen, H. Pierce, K. Palaniappan, and M. Manyin. NASA Goddard Lab for Atmospheres—data from National Oceanic and Atmospheric Administration NASA. **72** Photodisc/Getty Images **74–75** (b) Thomas Winz/Panoramic Images. **75** (t) Joseph Sohm/Corbis. **76** Tony Arruza/Corbis. **77** Terry Thompson/NGS Images.com/Panoramic Images. **78** Steve Dunwell/Getty Images. **79** Gibson Stock Photography. **80–81** (bkgd) Donovan Reese/Panoramic Images. **81** (tr) ABPL Image Library/Animals Animals/Earth Scenes. **86** (bl) Lonnie Duka/Index Stock Imagery; (br) Brad Wrobleski/Masterfile. **87** Alan and Sandy Carey/Photodisc Green/Getty Images. **94** C. C. Lockwood Bruce Coleman. **95** (tc) James Schwabel/Panoramic Images; (tl) New Moon/Panoramic Images; (tr) (c) HMCo./Photo Disk. **96** (br) Digital Vision. **96–97** (bkgd) Bryan Reinhart/Masterfile. **100** International Stock/Imagestate. **101** (br) Dwayne Newton/Photo Edit; (t) R. Ian Lloyd/Masterfile. **102** (l) Grant Heilman Photography; (r) Gibson Stock Photography. **104** Collart HERVE/Corbis. **105** (tl) Gibson Stock Photography; (tr) Gibson Stock Photography. **112–113** Banana Stock. **114** (r) Paul Barton/Corbis. **115** (r) Nik Wheeler/Corbis; (tl) Jerry Wachter/Photo Researchers. **116** Ariel Skelley/Corbis. **117** Tony Freeman/Photo Edit. **118** Lawrence Migdale. **119** (t) Dave G. Houser/Corbis. (b) David Bacon/The Image Works. **120** Courtesy of Aparna Agrawal; **121** Courtesy of Maria Carter; **122–123** (bkgd) North Wind Picture Archive. **123** (c) Bettmann/Corbis. **124** (b) Burke/Triolo/Retrofile; (t) Myrleen Ferguson Cate/Photo Edit. **125** (c) Claudia Kunin/Corbis; (l) Horace Bristol/Corbis; (r) Don Mason/Corbis. **126** Paul Barton/Corbis; (tr) Creatas. **127** (bl) Creatas; (c) David Young-Wolff/Photo Edit. **129** (b) Mark Gibson/Index Stock; (tl) Superstock. **132–133** (b) Osamu Honda/AP World Wide Photo; **133** (tr) AP World Wide Photos. **136** (b) Superstock. **136–137** (tl) Ken Davies/Masterfile. **137** (br) Thinkstock/Getty Images. **138** (b) ro-ma stock/Index Stock Imagery, Inc. **139** (b) Leif Skoogfors/Woodfin Camp & Associates; (t) Danny Lehman/Corbis. **140** (b) Craig Aurness/Corbis; (t) Photolink/Photodisc Green/Getty Images. **141** James P. Blair/Corbis. **142–143** (b) Richard T. Nowitz/Corbis. **143** (r) Photodisc/Getty Images. **144** (frame) © HMCo./C. Squared Studios/Photodisc/Getty Images; (frame) © HMCo./C. Squared Studios/Photodisc/ Getty Images; (l) Francis G. Mayer/Corbis; (r) Corbis. **145** Connie Ricca/Corbis. **146** (b) Roger Ressmeyer/Corbis; (c) Bob Krist/Corbis; (t) Michael Newman/Photo Edit. **147** Tim Boyle/Getty News and Sports/Getty Images. **148** (inset) Hulton Archive/Getty Images. **148–149** (bkgd) Walter P. Reuther Library, Wayne State University. **154** (c) Bob Thomas/Stone/Getty Images; (l) Jim Craigmyle/Corbis; (r) ImageState Pictor/PictureQuest. **156–157** David Young-Wolff/Photo Edit. **158** (l) Thinkstock/Getty Images; (r) Robert W. Ginn/Photo Edit. **160** Frank Siteman/Index Stock. **161** Superstock. **166** Photodisc/Getty Images. **167** LWA–Dann Tardif/Corbis. **168** (l) Jose Luis Pelaez, Inc./Corbis; (r) Ed Lallo/Index Stock Imagery. **169** (l) Stone/Getty Images; (r) Comstock Images. **172** Rogério Reis/Tyba Brazil Photos. **173** Corbis. **174** (bc) Scott Barrow/Image State; (r) Photo Researchers. **175** (cr) Photodisc/Getty Images; (tl) Albert Gustaf Aristeded Edelfelt/SuperStock. **176** (c) Photodisc/Getty Images; (cr) Photodisc/Getty Images; (tl) AP WorldWide Photos. **177** (l) Goldberg Diego/Corbis; (r) Goldberg Diego/Corbis. **178** G. K. & Vikki Hart/Getty Images. **181** (bl) Walter Hodges/Corbis; (br) © HMCo./C Squared Studios/Photodisc/Getty Images; (cr) Stone/Getty Images; (tl) John Coletti/Index Stock Imagery; (tr) Steve Cole/Photodisc/Getty Images. **182** Steve Dunwell/Indexstock Imagery. **183** Wonderfile. **188** (bl) Corbis; (br) Alan Pitcairn/Grant Heilman Photography; (c) Ed Young/Corbis. **189** (tr) Corbis. **191** (c) Taxi/Getty Images; (l) Ed Young/Corbis. **192** (l) Taxi/Getty Images; (r) Larry Lefever/Grant Heilman Photography. **193** David Young-Wolff/Photo Edit. **197** (tl) Allan Davey/Masterfile; (tr) Taxi/Getty Images. **198** (l) Dan Gair Photographic/Indexstock/PictureQuest; (r) Gibson Stock Photography. **208–209** John McGrail. **210** (l) The Bridgeman Art Library; (r) Maryann and Bryan Hempill/Index Stock. **211** (l) Bettmann/Corbis; (r) H.P. Merten/Zefa/Masterfile. **212** YVA Momatiuk & John Eastcott/Woodfin Camp & Associates. **216** (bl) Jules Frazier /Photodisc/Getty Images; (br) J. A. Kraulis /Masterfile; (tl) Scott T. Smith/Corbis; (tr) Marilyn "Angel" Wynn/NativeStock. **217** (tl) Marilyn "Angel" Wynn/Nativestock; (tr) Larry Ditto/Bruce Coleman. **222** The Granger Collection, New York. **223** The Bridgeman Art Library. **225** The Bridgeman Art Library. **226** Keren Su/Corbis. **228** John Anderson/Animals Animals. **242** Courtesy Don Troiani, Historical Military Imagebank. **244** Bettmann/Corbis. **245** (b) New York Historical Society/The Bridgeman Art Library; (t) Tom McHugh/Photo Researchers. **246** Photo Edit. **247** (tl) Massachusetts Historical Society. **248** Freelance Photography Guild/Corbis. **249** Rick Friedman/Corbis. **251** (c) Bettmann/Corbis; (frame) © HMCo./Image Farm; (l) Museum of the City of New York/Corbis; (r) Bettmann/Corbis. **253** The Bridgeman Art Library. **254** Bettman/Corbis. **255** Hulton Archive/Getty Images. **256** Bettman/Corbis. **257** Bettmann/Corbis. **258** (br) © HMCo./C Squared Studios/Photodisc/Getty Images; (cr) Bettman/Corbis. **259** Library of Congress. **260** Hulton–Deutsch Collection/Corbis. **262** (l) Underwood Photo Archives; (r) Minnesota Historical Society/Corbis. **263** (l) Underwood & Underwood/Corbis; (r) Courtesy of the Village of Plainfield. **264** (bl) Underwood & Underwood/Corbis; (tr) The Associated Publishers New York Public Library. **265** (bl) NASA/Science Source/Photo Researchers, Inc.; (tr) NASA. **266** (inset bl) George H.H. Huey/Corbis; (inset br) Bettmann/Corbis. **267** (bl) Bettmann/Corbis; (br) Mark M. Lawrence/Corbis; (cl) Hulton– Deutsch Collection/Corbis; (cr) Sean Sexton Collection/Corbis. **268** Tony Mc Grath/Hulton Archive/Getty Images. **269** (b) Underwood & Underwood Corbis; (t) Hulton Archive/Getty Images. **270** (br) Takaharu Yoshizawa/Photonica; (tl) Hot Idea's Collection/Index Stock. **271** Peter Cross's Collectiion/Index Stock. **272** (br) Museum of Mankind, London, UK/The Bridgeman Art Library. **272–273** (bkgd) Galen Rowell/Corbis. **274** (l) British Museum London/Art Resource, NY; (lc) Bettmann/Corbis; (r) Joseph Sohm/Corbis; (rc) Richard T. Nowitz/Corbis. **275** (bl) Richard T. Nowitz/Corbis; (lc) Archivo Iconografico, S.A./Corbis; (rc) Burstein Collection/Corbis; (tl) Colin Garratt; Milepost **92** 1/2/Corbis; (tr) Photonica. **276** The Granger Collection. **278–279** (l) Ariel Skelley/Masterfile. **280** (l) Rick Meyer/City of Burbank. **280–281** (b) © Getty Images. **281** (lc) Joseph Sohm Visions of America/Corbis. **282** Richard Hutchings/Photo Edit. **283** Paul Colangelo/CORBIS. **286** (c) Elena Rooraid/Photo Edit. (b) IndexStock Imagery **288–289** (bkgd) Skip Nall/Photodisc/Getty Images. **289** (inset) Chad Slattery/Stone/Getty Images. **301** Bonnie Kamin/Photo Edit. **302** © John Neubauer/Photo Edit. **303** Jose Carillo/Photo Edit. **304** Reuters NewMedia Inc./Corbis. **304–305** Bettmann/Corbis. **309** (br) Bell/Folio Inc.; (cr) AP World Wide Photos; (tr) Office of the Mayor, Columbus Ohio. **310** (cl) Steven Begleiter/Image State; (cr) Jim and Mary Whitmer. **311** Rick Friedman/Corbis. **317** The Granger Collection **318** Peter Gridley/Taxi/Getty Images. **319** (bl) Peter Gridley/Taxi/Getty Images; (tr) Doug Armand/Stone/Getty Images. **320** (br) Ghislain & Marie David de ossy/Imagebank/Getty Images; (tr) Index Stock. **321** (bl) Wilfredo Lee/AP Wide World Photo; (tr) Richard Hutchings/Photo Edit. **322** (b) AFP Corbis. **323** Wally McNamee/Corbis. **324** Mark Wilson/ Getty Images News and Sports/Getty Images. **325** (r) AFP/Corbis; (tl) Stephen Shaver, Pool/AP World Wide Photos. **326** (bl) Lawrence Migdale; (cl) Stockbyte/Punchstock. **327** (bc) David Young-Wolff/Photo Edit Inc; (c) Henryk T. Kaiser/Index Stock Imagery/Picturequest; (tc) Jack Star/Photolink/PhotoDisk/Getty Images; (tr) Dorian Weber/Index Stock Imagery.

Assignment Photography Credits

27 © HMCo./Ken Karp. **29** © HMCo./Ken Karp. **37** © HMCo./Ken Karp. **66–67** © HMCo./Ken Karp. **89–91** © HMCo./Ken Karp. **114** (l) © HMCo./Ken Karp. **128** © HMCo./Ken Karp. **130–131** © HMCo./Angela Coppola. **134** © HMCo./Ken Karp. **159** (r) © HMCo./Ken Karp. **180** © HMCo./Ken Karp. **184–185** © HMCo./Ken Karp. **187** © HMCo. **189** © HMCo./JP Maroot. **190** © HMCo./JP Maroot. **191** (r) © HMCo./JP Maroot. **227** (tr) © HMCO; (b) © HMCo./Ken Karp. **235–237** © HMCo./Ken Karp. **247** (bkgd) © HMCo./Angela Coppola. **252** © HMCo./Ken Karp. **267** © HMCo./Ken Karp. **284** © HMCo./Angela Coppola. **287** © HMCo./Angela Coppola. **292–293** © HMCo./Angela Coppola. **297–299** © HMCo./Angela Coppola. **308** © HMCo./Jade Albert. **312–315** © HMCo./Ken Karp. **328** © HMCo./Angela Coppola.

Illustration Credits

All cartographic maps done by Ortelious Design. **24** Ron Berg. **36** Alex Burnet. **43** Bob Depew. **46–47** Nathan Jarvis. **51** Christiane Beauregard. **58** Hector Borlasca. **60** Chris Lensch. **75–78** (borders) Sally Vitsky. **84** Mark and Rosemary Jarman. **86** Mark and Rosemary Jarman. **88–91** Steve Costanza. **92–93** Michael Maydak. **98** Jeffrey Mangiat. **103** Bob Depew. **108–109** Lucia Washburn. **151** Nathan Jarvis. **152** Promotion studios. **154** Nathan Jarvis. **162–163** Doris Barrette. **170–171** Len Ebert. **186** Peter Richardson. **194–195** Kathryn Mitter. **196** Lisa Campbell Ernst. **200** (br, cr) Jeffrey Mangiat. **204** Anthony Lewis. **214–215** Robert Van Nutt. **218–222** Richard Cowdrey. **230–233** Martha Aviles. **234–237** Jui Ishida. **239** Frank Riccio. **241** Viviana Diaz. **276** Leah Palmer Preiss. **284–285** Ortelius Cartography **294** Kathi Ember. **300** Ron Berg. **306** Jeff Mangiat. **310** Christiane Beauregard. **330** Nathan Jarvis.

Acknowledgments

For each of the selections listed below, grateful acknowledgment is made for permission to excerpt and/or reprint original or copyrighted material, as follows:

Permissioned Material

Excerpts from "*The Fire Fighter's Job*" and "*Brave Fire Fighters,*" from *The Fire Station,* by Stuart A. Kallen. Copyright © 1997 by Abdo Consulting Group, Inc. Reprinted by permission of Abdo Publishing Company.

"*God Bless America,*" by Irving Berlin. © Copyright 1938, 1939, © copyright renewed 1965, 1966 by Irving Berlin. © Copyright assigned to the Trustees of the God Bless America Fund. International Copyright Secured. All Rights Reserved. Reprinted by permission of the Irving Berlin Music Company.

Lyrics from "I Live in a City," words and music by Malvina Reynolds. Copyright © 1961 by Schroder Music Co. (ASCAP) Renewed 1989. Used by permission. All rights reserved.

Excerpt from "Jackie Robinson's letter to Branch Rickey," [1950], by Jackie Robinson, Copyright © Jackie Robinson. Reprinted by permission of The Jackie Robinson Foundation.

Excerpt from *Journey to Ellis Island: How My Father Came to America,* by Carol Bierman with Barbara Hehner. Text copyright © 1998 by Carol Bierman. Jacket copyright © 1998 by The Madison Press Limited. Reprinted by permission of Madison Press Books.

"Maple Talk," from *Poems Have Roots,* by Lilian Moore. Text copyright © 1997 by Lilian Moore. Reprinted with the permission of Atheneum Books for Young Readers, an imprint of Simon & Schuster Children's Publishing Division and Marian Reiner for the author.

Excerpt from "North" ("The Young Woman and the Thunder Beings"), from *Between Earth & Sky: Legends of Native American Sacred Places,* by Joseph Bruchac. Text copyright © 1996 by Joseph Bruchac. Reprinted by permission of Harcourt, Inc. and Barbara S. Kouts Agency.

Excerpt from "Our Family Comes From 'Round the World," from *Fathers, Mothers, Sisters, Brothers,* by Mary Ann Hoberman. Copyright © 1991 by Mary Ann Hoberman. Reprinted by permission of Little, Brown and Company, (Inc.) and Gina Maccoby Literary Agency.

Excerpt from *Raising Cows on the Koebels' Farm,* by Alice K. Flanagan. Copyright © 1999 by Alice K. Flanagan and Romie Flanagan. All rights reserved. Reprinted by permission of Children's Press, an imprint of Scholastic Library Publishing, Inc.

"Recess Rules," from *Lunch Money,* by Carol Diggory Shields, illustrated by Paul Meisel. Text copyright © 1995 by Carol Diggory Shields. Illustrations copyright © 1995 by Paul Meisel. Used by permission of Dutton Children's Books, a division of Penguin Young Readers Group, a member of Penguin Group (USA) Inc., 345 Hudson Street, New York, NY 10014. All rights reserved.

Excerpt from *Sheep on the Farm,* by Mari C. Schuh. Copyright © 2002 by Capstone Press. All rights reserved. Reprinted by permission of Capstone Press.

Excerpt from *Sheep Out to Eat,* by Nancy Shaw, illustrated by Margot Apple. Text copyright © 1992 by Nancy Shaw. Illustrations copyright © 1992 by Margot Apple. Reprinted by permission of Houghton Mifflin Company.

Excerpt from "South" ("The Great Smokies"), from *Between Earth & Sky: Legends of Native American Sacred Places,* by Joseph Bruchac. Copyright © 1996 by Joseph Bruchac. Reprinted by permission of Harcourt, Inc. and Barbara S. Kouts Agency.